THE IMPROVING ANNOTATOR

DAN HEISMAN

MONGOOSE
Press

BOSTON

Publisher: Mongoose Press
1005 Boylston Street, Suite 324
Newton Highlands, MA 02461
info@mongoosepress.com
www.MongoosePress.com
ISBN: 978-1-9362770-4-9
Library of Congress Control Number: 2010937584
Distributed to the trade by National Book Network
custserv@nbnbooks.com, 800-462-6420
For all other sales inquiries please contact the Publisher.

Layout: Semko Semkov
Editor: Jorge Amador
Cover Design: Creative Center – Bulgaria
Revised and expanded edition
0 9 8 7 6 5 4 3 2 1
Printed in China

Dedication

To my recently deceased, loving wife Holly. Without her never-ending trust in my abilities I could not have completed this book. Also, thanks so much for patiently putting up with my hours in front of the computer checking the analysis and typing the text. Holly's long and courageous fight against cancer at a young age is a reminder to us all to do the best we can. We'll all miss you, Nubes. This one's for you.

Acknowledgments

There are several people who helped make this book possible and a better product. I would like to acknowledge and thank the following:

Coach Donald Byrne, whose comments are provided in Games 14 and 16, and who provided inspiration for many chessplayers, including myself.

Eric Tobias, who suggested that a book about an improving annotator would be more meaningful if it included a section on annotating games.

Jorge Amador, whose patient reading helped make the text more readable and consistent – and twenty years later helped with the ideas for the updated edition.

Ernest Weaver, for helping to review the games added for this edition.

Bobby Dudley of Chess Enterprises, whose publication of my first book inspired me to put this one in publishable electronic format.

My second publisher, Mongoose Press, for encouraging this edition and making it available to a wider audience.

My late wife, Holly, and son, Delen, who tolerated Dad's hours at the computer and encouraged this project.

Index to Opponents, Opening, and Color

Symbols

+	Check
±	White is slightly better
∓	Black is slightly better
±	White is clearly better
∓	Black is clearly better
+−	White has a winning advantage
−+	Black has a winning advantage
#	Checkmate
=	The position is equal
∞	The position is unclear
∞̿	With compensation for the sacrificed material
≈	With approximately equal chances
!	A good move
!!	A brilliant move
!?	An interesting move
?!	A dubious move
?	A weak move
??	A blunder
□	A forced (only) move
△	With the idea of
✕	Weak point
⊕	Time trouble
1-0	White wins
0-1	Black wins
½-½	Draw

Introduction

"Annotating games will improve your play."

The unrated sixteen-year-old considered the advice. He knew he had gotten a late start in tournament chess and so decided to give it a try. First he annotated a match between two of his friends. Then, over the next three years, he annotated eighteen of his own games. He tried to be objective and to identify his weaknesses so as to not repeat his mistakes. In the first two years, his rating rose 600 points. In the third year, just after his nineteenth birthday, he became an expert.

That teenager was me, Dan Heisman. Eventually I won the Philadelphia Invitational Championship, got my national master (NM) title from the U.S. Chess Federation, and earned the Candidate Master (CM) title from the international chess federation, FIDE. This turned out to be my second book out of ten (!), and my *Novice Nook* column for Chess Café (www.chesscafe.com) has won several awards for Best Instruction.

I thought these games would make for an instructive book – *The Improving Annotator: From Beginner to Master*. The reader would be treated to good games, interesting positions, and very detailed annotations of complex situations. Since the unique aspect of this book is my improving annotation, the games are presented in the order I annotated them, not in the order they were played.

Only one problem remained. Now that I was a master, should I correct errors in my old notes? For the first 18 games, fixing the notes would destroy the reader's perception of the improving annotator, so I decided to leave them pretty much alone. (So when you see a game called "My Best Game," read it as "My Best Game *so far*.") I did convert these 18 to algebraic notation, made the text just a little more readable, but added a helpful note in brackets only occasionally. For the remainder of the games I did what all good annotators should do today *[i.e., 1995, publication date for the first edition – Ed.]*: double check the analysis of the most complex positions with chess software such as John Stanback's *Zarkov 3* or Mark Lefler's *NOW*.

These original and untouched errors in analysis are, hopefully, additionally instructive. As opposed to Bobby Fischer, I will not only not claim that I never made a mistake in analysis, I am somewhat proud of having tried so much and sometimes failed. This book is a testament to those mistakes – and to the learning process involved.

For this updated edition I have left the original games mostly untouched (else the book would not longer represent the notes of an

Improving Annotator); I did not correct my analysis mistakes. The main changes to those games were to fix a few typos and to add bracketed [new] comments. Most of these comments were generated by using 2009 World Computer Chess Champion *Rybka* to help the reader understand the "truth" of the position, especially in the more analytical lines. Comments based on *Rybka's* analysis are not only in brackets but also begin with "*R:*", e.g. "[*R:* This is the losing move. Black had to play 19...♖ac8, when 20.♖xa5 only gives White a slight advantage]."

Moreover, I used *Rybka* to completely re-analyze and annotate two of the most complicated games in the book (Yehl #10 and Latzel #14; for Dowling #18 see the Appendix of *Elements of Positional Evaluation*, 4th edition). The original annotations to the Yehl and Latzel games are still included, unaltered, but I have added a new section, "*Rybka* Redux," providing these games a second time with the new, computer-assisted annotations. In addition, I have provided two new games (Mucerino #27 and Rutar #28) to highlight my quest for the Main Line Chess Club Championship in recent years.

The method I use for computer analysis was described in detail in the introduction to my e-book/CD *The Traxler Counterattack*. Briefly, this is as follows: I do not just let the computer run overnight or use something like *Fritz's* "Overnight Analysis" mode. Instead, I put the engine in infinite analysis mode and painstakingly force the engine to show me the candidate moves. With my background as a chess master and in computer science, I am able to discern which variations are worth investigating. By doing this repeatedly, I create main lines for each critical variation. Some of the new annotations were created in this manner; for others I simply let the computer do a quick "blunder check."

For each game my objectives are the same: to find the truth, expose the errors, and let the reader know when and how the games were won and lost. Along the way I hope to be instructive as well. I trust you will enjoy playing through these games (and especially some of the fantastic tactical notes) as much as I enjoyed playing and annotating them.

Annotating a Chess Game

The improving self-annotator may annotate primarily to help him understand his own weaknesses and to try to avoid repeating any mistakes.

Any player wishing to improve should first ask their opponent to review the game with them immediately afterwards – the traditional "post-mortem." Only the opponent knows what he was thinking, so he can provide meaningful (and sometimes not so meaningful) insight into why his moves were chosen. But, more importantly, even opponents who are of equal strength or even somewhat inferior can provide important knowledge that you can use to improve. The opponent might understand the opening or endgame better, or he may have seen a particular line of analysis with deeper insight.

Assuming you wish to annotate the game, after reviewing the game with your opponent you can show it to a strong player for further examination, or analyze it in private prior to commiting any annotations to paper.

In these days of computer annotations, you should first annotate the game on a word processor (so that it can be modified later) *without the help of a computer chess program.*

Make sure to include clear evaluations of all lines using either symbols (=, ±) or words ("White is clearly better," or "Black is winning easily"). Never provide an analysis line leaving the reader wondering what the evaluation is.

After the first pass, use the computer to check your analysis and evaluations, making changes where necessary. By doing the annotation this way, it not only allows you to analyze without computer help (much more instructive), but it also forces you to review objectively what you have done, for double benefit.

If your original evaluation was one of "unclear," the engine will probably have a clear preference one way or another. Those are almost always instructive lines.

There are three main goals/purposes for annotating a game:

- Instruction

- Entertainment

- History

Any annotated game may contain one or more of these goals. Within each of these goals, subgoals may also differ.

The intended audience is also important. If these are fellow masters, then instructional material is extraneous and possibly even insulting. But the great majority of readers are not masters. Similarly, writing for intermediate players is vastly different from writing to instruct someone who has just learned the moves, or even writing for the general public. For this reason, writing for *New In Chess* magazine is different from writing *Novice Nook* (whose intended audience, ironically enough, *is* intermediates!), which is different from writing for the local newspaper.

First let's list considerations for annotating that are independent of the reason for annotation.

- Show all the points where the game changed from a win to a draw or loss, or a draw into a loss (the latter two are called "the losing move"); provide analysis of what could have been done instead. It is important to keep in mind the game theorem which states that, "your position can never get better when you make a move; your position is exactly as good as your best move." Of course, that doesn't mean there aren't good moves!

- If a move changes the expected result from a win to a draw, a win to a loss, or a draw to a loss, provide one or two question marks. A win to a loss usually deserves both question marks. Also, if a move turns a tough defense into a resignable position (or similarly turns a very easy victory or draw into a tough one), then this might also deserve question marks.

- Give a question mark – or maybe two in egregious cases – for "purposeful errors." For example, if a player trades down unnecessarily when losing, that violates a very important principle of resistance and may deserve more annotative scorn than a move which accidentally puts a queen *en prise* (which a player would not do on purpose).

- Award exclamation point(s) for:
    1) Any "hard to see" move which preserves the evaluation (win or draw).
    2) A move that creates great problems for the opponent, giving the mover a much better chance to win.
    3) A novel move which affects the evaluation of a known opening.
    4) A move which causes psychological problems for the opponent.

- Give a "!?" ("worth consideration") for a move which is not dubious, and purposely injects excitement or risk into the game.

- Give a "?!" for a move which is dubious but has some interest or is worth a try in difficult circumstances.

- Be objective. It is not credible to sprinkle the winner's moves with exclamation points and the loser's with question marks, especially if the winner wasn't winning throughout the whole game. In this book, especially as my opposition gets tougher, there are quite a few games where I started out with a disadvantage, and this I admit quite freely. Computers should help an annotator to be more objective.

- Provide both the time control and, if possible, how much time each player had left after each move. At the least you should provide this for your own moves (since it is helpful to have this information anyway when analyzing your games).

- When providing analysis, keep in mind the intended audience when deciding how much detail to provide. The general rule is:

  1) Strong players don't need everything pointed out to them; they know when one side or the other has the advantage and if you give them the first few moves of an alternative analysis, they get the picture.

  2) Beginners, on the other hand, do not need detailed lines either; they need very gentle, general instruction, with "guidelines" they can remember, such as "Putting Rooks on the seventh rank can be strong."

  3) The intermediate player, such as the average club player, is the toughest for whom to annotate. Each has his own strengths and weaknesses so, depending upon his knowledge, may sometimes need to be treated more like the strong player, and other times like a beginner. The intermediate player is often the type who likes the annotator to show the win "in all variations." I have leaned some of my annotations, especially my complicated games against Yehl (Game 10), Latzel (14), Dowling (18), and Lunenfeld (24) in this direction, showing most of the complicated (and usually entertaining) possibilities. For this reason, many of the diagrams in *The Improving Annotator: From Beginner to Master* show pretty analysis that was not played.

For *instruction,* supplementary considerations include:

- In the opening, discuss any new moves and, if the players do not follow best theory, let the reader know what is currently considered "best."

- Provide the time control and the time remaining after each move. This was done in some of my later games, as it gives insight into the players' thought process. It is important to know when the players are in time trouble. It is also important to be able to calculate how much time was taken on an individual move. A bad move made after 15 seconds of thought is a much different type of error than the exact same move made after 15 minutes of thought.

- Define terms appropriately. I have found that most players below intermediate level, no matter how experienced, erroneously believe that "winning the exchange" means "coming out ahead in a trade" rather than the chess-specific (and correct) meaning of "winning a rook for a bishop or knight." Therefore it is important, when writing for lower-level audiences, to carefully define terms that might be standard to a more practiced readership.

- Pick out places in the game where a general principle is exemplified or violated. State the principle and why the move does or does not comply, and the consequences. The more basic the audience, the more simple the principle that can be highlighted. The more advanced the audience, then not only the more subtle the principle, but also noting exceptions to principles can be very instructive. For example, with beginners it might make sense to emphasize, "Move every piece once before you move every piece twice, except if there is a tactic." For an intermediate readership, "This is the Carlsbad pawn formation where the famous minority attack with b4-a4-b5 can be played for White."

- When you make mistakes, do your best to explain why you made the mistake (played too fast, lack of tactical vision, got confused and forgot your earlier analysis, etc.). This can be highly instructive, especially if you are able to offer some advice to the reader on how they can avoid similar mistakes in their games!

For *entertainment*:

- Set the "scene" for the game, not necessarily to the detail you would for history (below), but in order to give the reader a feel for the motivations or feelings of one or both of the players.

- Keep notes brief, minimizing analysis.

- Highlight any "human" incidents that occurred during the game, especially those that provide insight or amusement.

- Pick out games and diagram positions that show amusing, or at least easily understood, continuations.

- Consider annotating game segments or problems. Since the purpose is not necessarily to instruct, the lack of the "big picture" is not too important.

Introduction

When providing *history*:

- Provide the setting for the game: Who, What, When, Where, and Why. Provide as many details as possible. For example, unlike entertainment or instruction, the round number is important and even the time of day may be pertinent.

- Discuss why the game was important to the players or others who may be involved. For example, it may be the next-to-last round and a player may have needed a win to stay in contention for first place, or to qualify for the grandmaster title.

- Put the "chess time period" in perspective so that readers of a later time period will understand the context of the situation, both on and off the board.

- Discuss the implications of the game results. For example, a Soviet junior game that led the loser to retire to oblivion and inspired the other to continue – and eventually to become world champion – is pertinent to history.

I hope this book will encourage the reader to consider self-annotation as part of any chess improvement program.

Dan Heisman
April 2010

My Ten Favorite Annotations

1. Game 21, Black's move 20: Why the best move wasn't played on purpose!

2. Game 14, Black's move 16: The thought process on why the desired plan didn't work.

3. Game 24, White's move 22 : How the win was missed after playing brilliantly, and how computer analysis found that missing win, improving on the defense as well!

4. Game 25, White's move 36: Why the computer's suggested move that wins material was rejected, and how the computer search window was used to find a better one.

5. Game 18, White's move 26: Shows quite a bit of analytical effort and tactical variations to prove that Black has a forced win after any move by White.

6. Game 10, White's move 16: Why disgust played a part in arriving at a very complicated, correct move.

7. Game 14, White's move 19: Again, lengthy tactical analysis proves how White could have saved the game.

8. Game 20, White's move 14: My opponent, writing in a magazine article, humorously explains how he felt about the opening.

9. Game 24, White's move 7: Describing a complete lapse in memory.

10. Game 19, Black's move 38: An unforgettable humorous exchange during the heat of a dual time scramble with Jack Peters.

Game 1:

Early Pawn Power

The U.S. Amateur is a popular national tournament which gives non-masters a chance to capture a national title. This game is a final-round encounter with Mrs. Mary Selensky, at the time the best of Philadelphia's female players. (Mrs. Selensky, a solid 1800 player, scored her biggest success later that year by coming in third in the U.S. Women's Invitational Championship.) This tournament was my first strong national event, and my 4-3 score was good enough for 76th place out of about 220 and a gain of about 85 rating points.

Mary Selensky (1800) – Dan Heisman (1467)
U.S. Amateur, Philadelphia 1967
English Opening

1.c4 ...

This, the English, is a favorite of a few Philadelphia players, among them D. Spiro and L. Segal.

1... e5

In my early encounters against the English, this was my automatic reply. Today (at the time of the annotation) I consider this to be playing into White's hands, especially after an opening debacle against Mr. W. Toikka at Bloomsburg 1967, which I luckily managed to draw.

2.♘c3 ♘f6
3.g3 ...

Spiro also enjoys this line, a sort of Sicilian Dragon reversed.

3... ♘c6
4.♗g2 ♗b4

An opening irregularity, ceding the center and the bishop pair. This continuation was nicely refuted by Spiro in my game against him two months later.

5.♘f3(?) ...

Inferior to Spiro's e4.

5... ♗xc3
6.dxc3 ...

1

This leads to an entirely different game than 6.bxc3.

6...	d6
7.O-O	♗e6

Always looking for adventure (and usually finding trouble), I prepare to castle queenside, where I have a pawn majority, hoping for a wild game.

8.b3	h6

With the black bishop on e6 and her queen's bishop not developed, this takes away one of White's most important squares with the added power of starting a kingside roller with a tempo. After the game Mrs. Selensky admitted that this move seemed exceptionally strong to her. The mechanical 8...♕d7 or 8...♕e7 is too passive.

9.e3?	...

Mrs. Selensky touched the pawn, meaning to move it to e4 but, realizing that it was *en prise* there, had to settle on e3, where it blocks in the queen's bishop and relegates White to passivity.

9...	♗g4

Allowed by White's last move, this forces an ultimately fatal weakness in the white kingside.

10.h3	...

This must be played now, or else 10...e4 could not be met by the customary 11.h3 because of simply 11...exf3, winning a piece.

10...	♗e6
11.♖e1	♕d7
12.♔h2	...

There was nothing better.

12...	O-O-O

With his advantage, Black could play it safe and castle kingside, but he goes ahead with his earlier plan.

13.e4	...

I doubt if this is a case for "better late than never."

13...	♖dg8
14.♘g1??	...

The losing move. [Bad, but not that bad; only one question mark is deserved.] I had been trying to think of how to dislodge the knight, but Mrs. Selensky makes it easy. My whole plan had revolved around a way to achieve this dislodgement. She probably either wanted to relocate the knight or push the f-pawn, both of which must be to Black's advantage.

14...   **h5**

This looks unnatural, but it contains a deadly threat.

15.f4?   **...**

[This is more likely the losing move. *Rybka* thinks 15.♗f1 was far superior, when after 15...g5 Black is better but not necessarily winning.]

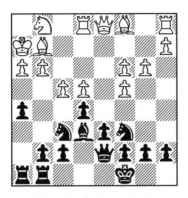

Position after 15.f4?

Although this threatens to win the bishop, she misses the not so obvious:

15...   **♘g4+ −+**

This was the third time I had put a piece *en prise* to a pawn in the tournament. Twice it worked, but the third time I missed a winning line.

16.hxg4   **...**

Forced. If 16. ♔h1, then 16...♘f2+ wins the queen.

16...   **hxg4+**
17.♘h3   **...**

If 17.♗h3 (threatening f4-f5), simply 17...f6 or 17...♕e7 is sufficient for Black because the bishop on h3 won't run away.

17...   **gxh3**
18.♗f3   **...**

Of course, if 18.f5, then 18...hxg2+ followed by ...♗xf5 is more than enough.

18... exf4

19.gxf4 ...

White's king is now looking mighty lonely. The combination starting with 15...♘g4+ has also won a pawn.

19... ♕e7

Saving the bishop and threatening 20...♕h4 and then ...♕f2+.

20.♖g1 ♕h4

21.♗e3 ...

Developed at last. Here, the fatal consequences of 9.e3 can be seen.

21... ♘e7

The knight wishes to join in on the kingside "fun."

22.♕e2 f5?

Black finally makes a serious error, allowing White counterplay. I was trying to open up the kingside. Of course, White cannot play 23.♗xa7 because of 23...b6, trapping the bishop.

23.e5?? −+ ...

After this, White's game becomes untenable. 23.e5 actually justifies Black's last move. Simply 23.exf5 is strong, opening diagonals for the bishops. If 23...♘xf5, White has 24.♗f2 or even 24.♗xa7 if nothing else, because of the discovery on Black's bishop. If 23...♗xf5, then 24.♗f2 ♕f6 (forced) followed by 25.♗d4 is just one reasonable line at White's disposal.

23... dxe5

24.fxe5 g5

Is that three connected passed pawns I see marching upon White's naked king in the early middlegame?!

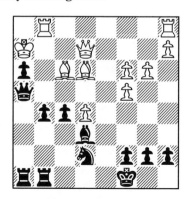

Position after 24...g5

25.≝ad1 ...

This loses quickly, but there wasn't much to be done.

25... **g4**
26.≗xg4 ...

White must lose a piece. If 26.≗h1?? g3+ and mate next move.

26... **fxg4**
27.≗f2 ...

Now at least opposite colored bishops allow White to do some blockading.

27... **♕g5**
28.≝d4 **♘g6**

Threatening 29...♘f4.

29.♗g3? ...

There goes the blockade.

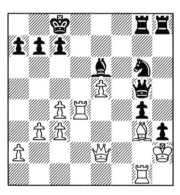

Position after 29.♗g3?

29... **♘h4**

Of course. The threat of ...♘f3+ with a double fork, winning material, forces the following exchange:

30.♗xh4 **♕xh4**
31.≝g3 ...

To stop 31 ...g3+.

31... **♕g5**

On 31... ♕xg3+ 32.♔g3 h2, White can simply play 33.♖d1 and the outcome would be delayed.

32.a4 ...

Might as well try a pawn-roller. Of course, White neglects Black's infiltration while doing so.

32...	**♖f8**
33.a5	**♕c1**
34.a6	...

34.♖d1 was "better," but Black could then try 34...♖f7+ with what appears to be a quicker win.

34... **♖f1**

White can resign. It was Sunday and the trains to my suburban home were only running every few hours. It was now nearing the time I had to leave in order to make the next train, but I felt it was impolite – and possibly counterproductive – to inform my opponent of my desire not to extend the game longer than reasonable. Besides, my opponent had no way of knowing her opponent would not play like a 1400 player, who would normally have the possibility of messing up royally.

35. ♖3xg4 ...

Desperation.

35...	**♖h1+**
36.♔g3	**♖g1+**
37.♔h2	**♗xg4**
38.axb7+	**♔b8**

The simplest and safest.

39.♖xg4 ...

With the extra piece attacking g5 via ... ♖h1+ and ...♖g1+, Black prevented the white queen from capturing on move 38 with check.

39... **♖h1+**

There are undoubtedly quicker wins, but I was playing at lightning speed, hoping to catch my train. Unfortunately, my opponent must have been upset that I was trying to speed things up, so she had now slowed down to five minutes a move!

40.♔g3 **♕e1+**

Five minutes later...

41.♕xe1   **♖xe1**
42.♔h2   **...**

Resigning is sometimes hard.

42...   **♖e2+**
43.♔h1   **h2**

The aliens have now convinced my opponent that "Resistance is Futile."

0-1

I missed my train.

Game 2

Can You Do That?

I was a lowly C player who had been playing for less than a year. My opponent was Mike Kubacki, a high A player (I had never beaten someone rated over 1900 to that time) generally acknowledged as Pennsylvania's top high school player of 1967. I felt overmatched. But Mike got into his habitual time trouble – even at 40/2 – and decided to sacrifice a rook for a murderous attack. Just when I was deciding to sacrifice my queen for purposes of survival, I realized the refutation was to make a move to which many players would reply, "Can you do that?!"

Mike Kubacki (1900) – Dan Heisman (1467)
LaSalle Invitational, Philadelphia 1967
Sicilian Defense

| 1. e4 | c5 |
| 2.♘f3 | a6 |

The O'Kelly System, my pet at the time, was borrowed from a player from our rival high school (Upper Moreland), Andy Kuntz. I achieved fair success with it until positionally crushed by Don Latzel at the Philadelphia Open Championship later in 1967 – even though Don employed it himself in the next round and won!

3.♘c3 ...

An unusual way of meeting the O'Kelly. Clarence Kalenian, former U.S. Amateur Champion, when faced with this move transposes into the Taimanov Variation with 3...e6. Most usual for White is 3.d4, although in his opening book GM Luděk Pachman gives this move a "?". 3.d4 is not that bad, but 3.c4 and 3.c3 relegate 2...a6 to a wasted tempo, and are therefore better.

3... b5?!

This is a diehard O'Kelly move, recommended to me by NM Rich Pariseau, should I wish to continue in "pure" O'Kelly lines. I have seen the move at least one other time.

4.g3 ...

The game is completely independent now, which is fine with me owing to Kubacki's slow play, usually leading to him being in time pressure.

4...   **e6**

Another pawn move, but I must block up the holes in my light squares.

5.♗g2   **♗b7**
6.d3   **...**

While trying to recreate this game without my notes (remembering is usually fairly easy for a memorable game), I thought O-O was Kubacki's 6th move, but if this had been played, then after 6...b4 and 7...♗xe4 I might be able to weather the storm a pawn up.

6...   **♞e7**

I am aiming at an early ...d7-d5 with an initiative, although I am admittedly down in development.

7.O-O   **d5**
8.exd5   **...**

Best. The half-open e-file is to White's advantage, especially in view of my early ["youthful"] aversion to castling because it "loses a tempo," a common beginner's fault.

8...   **♞xd5**

I was looking for a couple of exchanges to catch up in development, but not looking for too many exchanges, because I wanted to keep the game complicated.

9.♞xd5(?)   **...**

Trading knights is possibly not best. He should not fear doubled pawns here, so developing the queen bishop is best, even if to d2.

9...   **♛xd5?!**

For two moves I suffered under the delusion that the f3-knight was pinned because of mate. Of course, 10.♞h4 or 10.♞e1 forces 10...♛d7, a loss of tempo.

10.♖e1   **...**

Aha! A waiting policy – or so I thought.

10...   **♗e7**

9

Of course, if 10...♘d7?? 11.♘h4 wins a piece.

11.♘h4   ...

About this point I realized my mistake and hastened to move:

11...   **♕d7**

12.♕g4 ±   ...

Partly because of Black's dubious 9th move, White has a rather large advantage, but he had used about an hour, almost half his time for the entire game! I was determined to keep things complicated.

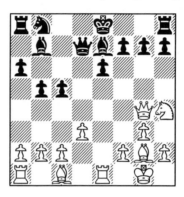

Position after 12.♕g4

12...   **g6**

On 12...O-O, 13.♗h6 should win, even if Black temporarily defends with 13...♗f6.

[Incorrect. *Rybka* says 12...O-O is clearly best, and after 13.♗h6 ♗f6=.]

13.♗g5 would also be strong. 12...♔f8 looks naturally bad, and the immediate 12...♗f6 can be met by 13.♘f5! Of course, 12...♗xh4? would leave Black fatally weak on the dark squares.

13.♘f3   ...

Headed for e5 or g5.

13...   **♘c6**

Still resolved to keep pieces on the board.

14.♗d2   ...

Threatening 15.♗c3, which, if Black now "passed," should win. However, the immediate 14.♗h6 or 14.♗g5 is more aggressive.

14...   ♗f6

Forced to prevent the aforementioned 15. ♗c3.

15.c3?!   ...

Having the following sacrifice in mind already – with about 40 minutes or less to go.

15...   ♛xd3

I accept the challenge in a Ken-ful manner. [A reference to my college roommate, Ken Boehm, who endorsed GM Larry Evans's pawn-snatching style. *Rybka* prefers 15...O-O with a slight advantage for White.]

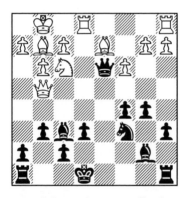

Position after 15...♛xd3

16.♖e6+??!   ...

A forceful sacrifice, similar to those found in Tal's early games. Here, however, it cannot be sound, theoretically because of the number of Black pieces in the defensive area and practically because of White's time trouble ⊕. [*Rybka* says 16.♗g5! is best with a clear White advantage.]

16...   fxe6
17.♛xe6+   ♗e7

Why not save all the pieces? [*R:* 17...♘e7 is much better, when Black is essentially winning.]

18.♘e5?   ...

Although this has sundry threats (queen checks, ♘xc6, ♗xc6, etc.), it cannot be good because of its "tradeful" nature and the fact that the bishop is hanging on d2. 18.♖e1 may be better. [I was wrong again. *Rybka* says that 18.♘e5! is clearly best, when Black should only be slightly better with best play.]

18...   **♘xe5**

Why not?

19.♕xe5   **...**

A hard choice. On 19.♗xb7 ♖a7 and both bishops hang. [*Rybka* thinks 19.♕xe5? loses. Best is 19.♗xb7! and play should continue 19... ♕xd2 20.♕xe5 O-O with a slight Black advantage.]

19...   **♗xg2!**

I'll take 'em all. Now 20.♕xh8+ fails against 20...♔d7 and either the other white bishop falls or the black bishop on g2 survives, with eventual mate threats for Black.

20.♖e1 ⊕   **...**

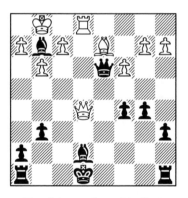

Position after 20. ♖e1

Best. [Not true. Objectively, 20.♕xh8 is better but White is still losing. So perhaps a better annotation is, "The best try."]

With now less than 10 minutes to play, White gives Black a difficult problem. If now 20...♖a7 21.♕xh8+ will work. The same applies to 20... ♕d7, blocking the king's escape square. White also threatens the black bishop and ♗g5. I contemplated the continuation 20...♗e4?? 21.♖xe4 ♕xe4 22.♕xe4, giving back the material. If I could only stop the attack, any endgame would be easily won for me. Suddenly, I realized that I had a simple problem-type move which solved all my worries. I simply played:

20...   **O-O-O! −+**

Now the white bishop must fall, leaving Black a rook up, and my king has "room to roam." [*Rybka* agrees, and notes that 20...O-O is even better, but in both cases castling wins.]

21.♕xe7   **♕xd2**

No qualms now.

22.♕xc5+   **♔b8**

If now 23.♕b6+, then 23...♗b7 24.♖e7 ♕d1+ is mate. So...

23.♖e7   **...**

Threatening some mates, but I easily foresaw the simplification:

23...   **♕d1+(!)**
24.♔xg2   **♕d5+**
0-1

The endgame finds Black a rook up. This game won me the upset prize, but I didn't win another game the rest of the tournament (1 win, 1 draw, 2 losses).

Game 3

Who Needs a Queen?

This game proved very satisfying to the first-year player. It was only the second 1800 player I had ever beaten, but moreso it was my first aesthetically pleasing game. Not only was it my first "queen-sacrifice" game, but it proved to be the first game I had played which attracted a large "post-mortem" audience. This was also my first published game (in the Pennsylvania state chess magazine, *Pennswoodpusher*)!

Dan Heisman (1467) – John Davies (1700)
Philadelphia Open Championship, Philadelphia 1967
French Defense

1.e4   ...

At this point, my play is truly the equal of Fischer's.

1...   e6

And John Davies's of Robert Byrne's!

2.d4   d5
3.♘c3   ...

In these "pre-Tarrasch variation" days, I used to have interesting games. Although I lost more frequently with 3.♘c3 than with Tarrasch's 3.♘d2, I probably shall return to it for the excitement!

3...   ♗b4

The Winawer Variation, a favorite of many 20th Century players, including Aron Nimzowitsch.

4.e5   c5
5.a3   ♗xc3+
6.bxc3   ...

All "pre-book" formalities.

6...   ♕a5(?)

This is the beginning of Black's troubles. The customary moves now are 6...♘e7 or 6...♕c7. The trouble with the text is that the queen is temporarily banished to the queenside for a while – watch her the rest of the game.

7.♗d2 ...

I now "pin" this bishop, for if it should move needlessly, ...♕xc3+ and ...♕xa1 would be detrimental to White's chances. The bishop never moves, but he could (should!) have – you'll see what I mean at the end of the game.

7... **c4(?)**

Another weak move, Black is confusing the opening with *MCO*, page 156 Column 46 [Note from many years later: This is the way we used to talk, when *Modern Chess Openings 10* was the opening bible!], which runs 1.e4 e6 2.d4 d5 3.♘c3 ♗b4 4.e5 c5 5.a3 ♗xc3 6.bxc3 ♘e7 7.♘f3 ♕a5 8.♗d2 c4. The big difference is that Black defers ...♕a4 and ...c5-c4 until after White commits himself to ♘f3, thus blocking off White's possible move ♕g4. Better is 7...♕a4.

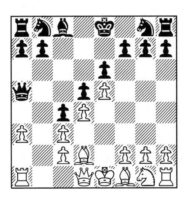

Position after 7...c4(?)

8.♕g4 ...

Black now has a sorry choice. He can hurt his pawn structure and weaken the dark squares with ...g7-g6 or play the thematic two-pawns sacrifice with ...♘g8-e7 in a position where the center is closed.

8... **♘e7?**

He chooses the latter plan, which does not prove particularly strong. This is probably the losing move!

9.♕xg7 **♖g8**
10.♕xh7 **♘d7**

The first of ten(!) consecutive knight moves for Black. Does anyone know a similar game where so many consecutive knight moves were made so early in the game by one player?

11.h4?! ...

This passed pawn proves strong and an important psychological edge. However, I made this move under the misconception that I was threatening 12.♗g5, with the idea of ♗xe7 and ♕xg8, but of course the bishop is still "pinned."

11... ♘f8

Gaining development by attacking the queen.

12.♕h5 ♘8g6

This knight is to play a poor role.

13.♘f3 ...

On the other hand, the white knight will play an important role on the weakened dark squares.

13... ♘f4??!

Possibly hoping for 14.♗xf4?? ♕xc3+ and 15...♕xa1. This kind of move is aesthetically pleasing to the one making it, but when considering such pleasing moves one must also make sure it is not "chessically" weak.

14.♕h6 ♘4g6

Just the point! When analyzing my 14th move, I rejected Black's 14... ♘xg2+? because of 15.♗xg2 ♖xg2 16.♖g1:

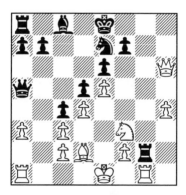

Position after 16.♖g1 (analysis)

forcing the exchange of rooks, and thereafter the passed pawn would probably cost Black a knight, and there are other good lines after 14... ♘xg2+? for White as well due to Black trading off his kingside defenders.

15.h5 ...

White's attack is very strong at any rate.

15... ♘f5

This *Zwischenzug* (in-between move) turns out badly, but nothing is much better. If 15...♖h8 16.♕g5 ♘f8, then 17.♕h4 and White can play g2-g4 or ♘g5 with winning effect. Lines with h5-h6 are also possible. On 15...♘f8, White can play the same kind of lines (as in ♕h4) with even more effect.

16.♕g5 ♘6e7

Forced, of course.

17.♕f4(?) ...

One of my two great regrets from this game. The game variation is a strong and forcing one, however, during the game I properly analyzed 17.♕f6!, which I rejected because I was winning anyway and didn't want to lose my queen in case I misanalyzed the main, extremely interesting line: 17...♖g7 18.h6 ♘g8 and now White can play 19.hxg7! ♘xf6 20.exf6! (see diagram) and wins easily. By the way, if Black does not go for this line, 17.♕f6 threatens 18.♘g5.

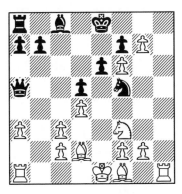

Position after 20.exf6! (analysis)

17... ♘c6

Forced! The threat was 18.g4 ♘g7 19.h6 and the knight is lost. Thus, his brother must make room for him at e7.

18.g4   ♘5e7
19.♘g5   ♘d8

At the time, I thought this was best; however, 19...♖f8 holds out longer, though after 20.♘h7 ♖h8 21.♕h6 threatening ♕g7 and ♘f6+ is strong. Of course, if 19...♖g7, 20.h6 wins immediately.

20.♘h7   ♖h8

This loses prettily. However, if 20...♖g7, one winning line is 21.♘f6+ ♔f8 22.h6 and wins. However, now White notices a spectacular mate in three, which I stupidly announce – my other great regret in this game being not able to see the mate take place on the board – and make the first move:

21.♘f6+   **1-0!**

I announced 21...♔f8 22.♕h6+!! ♖xh6 23.♗xh6# (see diagram). A pure bishop and knight mate in the middlegame by a 1400 player!

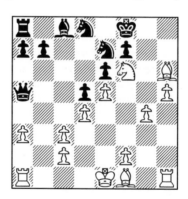

Final (unplayed!) position after 23.♗h6 mate!

Other unusual aspects about this game:

- After 7...c4(?), Black made only knight and king's rook moves.

- After 9...♖g8, Black made ten(!) consecutive knight moves!

- The "pinned" bishop was to do the mating: very pleasing – sacrificing the queen to "unpin" the bishop.

- There were no bishop moves after the opening.

- Black's queen remained still after 6... ♕a5(?). He should have played the thematic 7...♕a4 immediately (instead of 7...c4?) with a decent game.

Game 4

Here, Have Two!

Together with Game Three, this game helped me achieve the feat of beating two "A" players in one weekend, an encouraging accomplishment for me at the time. Shortly after the opening, my opponent must have diagnosed his position as desperate, for he sacrifices a piece for two pawns. Unfortunately for him, lines were only opened up for me, allowing me to pull off a return sacrifice to break up the pawns plus a second sacrifice, thus: "Here, have two!"

Dan Heisman (1467) – R. Taylor (1800)
Philadelphia Open Championship 1967
Sicilian Defense

1.e4	c5
2.♘f3	♘c6
3.d4	cxd4
4.♘xd4	d6
5.♘c3	g6

My first encounter with the Dragon. I have had good success in taming it. [Note: This order of moves is not usual because the omission of an early ...♘f6 gives White the option of playing c2-c4 with a Maróczy Bind position.]

6.♗e3	♗g7
7.♕d2	♘f6
8.f3	...

The Yugoslav Attack, or Dragon Killer, is a method I picked up from Ken Boehm, then first board at my arch-rival high school, Upper Moreland (Pennsylvania). At the time, I knew nothing about the Dragon except Ken's advice: "Play f3, castle queenside, and throw your kingside pawns at him!"

8...	0-0
9.0-0-0	...

At this point, I did not realize that 9.♗c4 was considered better, for after 9.0-0-0 Black has the choice of two good variations:

A) 9...♘xd4 10.♗xd4 ♗e6, or

B) 9...d5, sacrificing a pawn for open lines and the attack.

9...   **a6**

This is not usual, but in *MCO-10* page 194, column 39, note (1) it gives 9...a6 10.g4 ♘xd4 11.♗xd4 ♗e6 transposing into note *f*, which is the best line for Black. However, I still consider that ...♕c7 in these lines is a better idea for Black, e.g., 9...♘xd4 10.♗xd4 ♗e6 11.♔b1 ♕c7!.

10.g4   **...**

Going along with the plan.

10...   **♖e8? ±**

After the game, this move was roundly condemned, and rightly so. It has no part in the system. 10...♘xd4 was relatively best.

11.h4   **...**

Here they come, and now, why not?

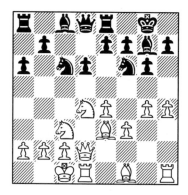

Position after 11.h4

11...   **♘xg4? +−**

This sacrifice is surely unsound. It leads to no Black play if White continues properly. [*Rybka* thinks the three best ideas for Black, all in contention for best, are 11...♘xd4 12.♗xd4 ♗e6 13.h5; 11...♘d7 12.h5; or 11...h5 12.♘xc6 bxc6 13.e5!. In each case White is much better but perhaps not winning.]

12.fxg4   **♗xg4**
13.♗e2   **...**

Since ♗f1-c4 wasn't played, this move is handy and natural.

13...   **♗xe2**
14.♘3xe2   **...**

There is nothing wrong with this capture, although 14.♘4xe2 was more accurate because it removes Black's pressure on this piece, freeing White's pieces while preventing ♘xd4 for good. However, both of White's knights are destined for starring roles.

14...   **h5**

Else 15.h5 is very strong.

15.♗h6   **♗h8**

On 15...♗xh6 16.♕xh6, White follows with 17.♘f5!, or on 16...e6 17.➓g1 threatens ♕xh5. Black is probably lost in any case, so he may as well keep pieces on the board.

16.➓hg1   **...**

Storm clouds gather.

16...   **♘e5**
17.♘f4!   **...**

To make this move, I actually had to envision the rest of the game (for all practical purposes)!

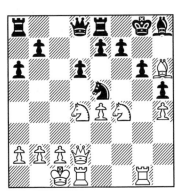

Position after 17.♘f4!

17...   **♘g4**

White now launches a tremendous attack.

18.♘xh5 ...

The threat is 19.♖xg4. On 18...♘xh6 19.♕xh6 wins a pawn with more to come. On 18...♗xd4 19.♖xg4.

18... **gxh5**
19.♕g5+ **♔h7**
20.♕xh5! ...

Black has no defense against 21.♖xg4 and mate, e.g., 20...♘f6 21.♕xf7+ ♔xh6 22.♕g6#, or 20...♘e5 21.♗f4#, or 20...♗g7 21.♗xg7+ ♔xg7 22.♖xg4+ ♔f6 23.♕f5#.

20... **♘xh6**

The crucial line to calculate, as the second piece is sacrificed.

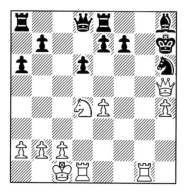

Position after 20...♘xh6

21.♘f5! ...

The quiet move. This is the move I had to foresee on my 17th move. There is no defense to ♕xh6 mate. If 21...♗g7 22.♖xg7+ ♔h8 23.♕xh6#, so:

21... **♗xb2+**

Sheer desperation.

22.♔b1 ...

I did not want to allow any checks.

22... **♗c1**
23.♔xc1 **1-0**

Game 5

Endgaming the Endgamer

In the worst (comparatively speaking) tournament of my life, the South Jersey Amateur 1967, I scored 2-4. This game was my only shining light. In my opponent's previous game, he had objected to adjudication because he felt he could outplay my (then) low-rated friend, Dave Wetzell, because he (Mr. Hauck) "lives for the endgame." Thus, I was wary to go into the endgame against him, but I converted my slight advantage into a large one by "endgaming the endgamer."

Dan Heisman (1500) – S. Hauck (1859)
South Jersey Amateur, Camden 1967
Blackmar-Diemer Gambit

1.d4   ...

If I'm not strong, at least I'm versatile!

1...   ♘f6

My opponent thinks we're going to play an Indian system. The surprise was on him.

2.f3?!   ...

The first signal of the speculative Blackmar-Diemer Gambit. Although I never lost a tournament game with this opening in about a half-dozen tries, I gave it up because it gave lower-rated players too much chance for an upset. [Note: I later lost a game with the BDG to multi-time Pennsylvania state champion Mike Shahade.] However, I did score some nice victories with the BDG, including this upset over a then much higher-rated opponent.

2...   **d5**

My opponent accepts the challenge to stop e2-e4 and play along classical lines. He could still transpose into the Sämisch variation of the King's Indian or into a Pirc system by playing 2...g6 or 2...d6.

3.e4?!   ...

The typical Blackmar-Diemer "thrust."

23

3...	**dxe4**
4.♘c3	**exf3**

Transposing into "normal" lines which usually begin 1.d4 d5 2.e4 dxe4 3.♘c3 ♘f6 4.f3 fxe4.

5. ♕xf3?! ...

The most complicated capture. 5.♘xf3 seems more natural, but has less involved lines and White seems to get less for the pawn. [Reminder: This was my opinion written not so long after this 1967 game, when I was still at best a "B" (1600-1800) player!]

5... **c6**

Guarding the important b-pawn and avoiding the complicated 5... ♕xd4(?) lines, one of the prettiest which runs 6.♗e3 ♕b4(?) 7.O-O-O ♗g4(?) 8.♘b5!! and White won all fifteen games in *Chess Charts*. [A 1960's book showing the results of each variation as it occurred in a database of thousands of master games. Of course, if a line was previously thought to be winning and later refuted by one new move, it may have won 90% of the time, yet lose by force! Still, the probabilities given were pretty informative, and one can get similar information electronically from ChessBase or other electronic databases today.] Black's natural play is often disastrous in this unnatural line.

6.♗e3 ...

This and 6.♗d3 are played.

6...	**♗g4**
7.♕f2	**e6**
8.h3	...

All this is still "book," or rather "chart," with the chart showing that White won three out of four games.

8... **♗f5**

8...♗h5 is usually played. The text enables White to castle immediately. [*Rybka* prefers 8...♕b6, when it thinks White has relatively little to show for his pawn sacrifice.]

9.O-O-O **♘e4(?)**

Certainly Black should try to simplify, but he is losing more tempi, which is what he has least. [*Rybka* judges 9...♘d5 to be best, when White has a lot to prove to show that his pawn sacrifice is sound.]

10.♘xe4 **♗xe4**

11.♗c4   ...

The text prevents. 11...♕d5 with a double attack on the a- and g-pawns. If now 11...♗d5 12.♖f1 and Black is in serious difficulty.

11...   **b5**
12.♖f1!   ...

This *Zwischenzug* allows Black the opportunity to go wrong...

12...   **♗g6(?)**

Which he does. Black's text allows White's answer, which was not practical before. [*Rybka* rates 12...♕f6! best, with Black still clearly on top.]

13.♗d3   ...

Threatening to win a piece.

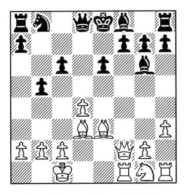

Position after 13.♗d3

13...   **f6(?)**

Black is making things hard on himself, although a queen move (to protect f7 after the bishops are traded) can be answered by 14.♗xg6, 15.♘f3, and 16.♘e5. Also, 13...♕e7 hampers the black bishop on f8, 13...♕d7 the knight on c8, and 13...♕c7 [which *Rybka* thinks is best with an equal game.] allows a later ♗f4-e5.

14.♗xg6   **hxg6**

White is piling up small advantages.

15.♘e2   **♕a5**

Black tries to stir up queenside action, but all he does is loosen up his pawns for the endgame. [*R:* much better is 15...♘a6, with an almost equal game.]

16.♔b1   **b4?!**
17.♘f4   **♔f7**

The king is probably safer here than anywhere else.

18.♖e1   **...**

This rook will put pressure on e6 while the other rook replaces him. [*Rybka* strongly prefers 18.♕g3, when it evaluates White as likely winning after 18...g5 19.♘d3.]

18...   **♗d6**
19.♗d2   **♗xf4**

Again Black tries to relieve the pressure by exchanges. He must stop 20.♘xe6, of course. Now his dark squares become weak.

20.♕xf4   **...**

Keeping the black queen and knight bottled up.

20...   **♘d7?**

Missing White's threatened reply. [*R:* Better is 20...♖d8, but 20... ♘d7 is just about as good and does not deserve a question mark.]

21.♕d6   **...**

With threats on three pawns, Black must return one. [*R:* 21.♕g3 was more accurate.]

21...   **♕d5**

Undoubtedly best.

22.♗xb4   **♕xd6**
23.♗xd6   **...**

Position after 23.♗d6

Let's look at the endgame: White has a queenside majority and a fine post for his bishop at c5, should the knight ever move. Black has two isolated pawns and doubled pawns. White controls the center and his king is safer, thus he has a winning advantage. But this is not enough to win. One must either convert his advantage into a win or talk his opponent into resigning. I took the easier course (the former!).

23...   **♖h4**
24. c3   **...**

24.g4, the alternative, puts a backward pawn on an open file and ties down the white rook on h1.

24...   **♘b6**

Black gives the bishop his outpost in return for a temporary spot for his knight at c4.

25.♖e2   **...**

White plans to pressure the e-pawn.

25...   **♘c4**
26.♗c5   **a5?**

Still trying for queenside action. Another purpose of 25.♖e2 is to protect the b-pawn. However, the text loses a pawn in the form of a combination. [According to *Rybka,* this is the losing move. Much better is 26...♖e4, when White has some pull but Black should hold.]

27.b3   **...**

[I missed 27.♖he1 winning, when 27...♖e8 fails to 28.b3 and Black can only save his knight with 28...♖b8 29.♖xe6 +−.]

27...   **♖b8**

At the time seemingly forced, although at the time of this annotation it looks like 27...♖e4!? is worth considering. [*Rybka* concurs: Black is worse but may hold. Now it is all over.]

28.♔c2   **♘b6**
29.♖1e1(?)   **...**

White has gained the needed time to win the e-pawn. However, 29 ♗xb6 first was more accurate because it prevents the doubling of White's pawns.

29...   **♘d7**

30.♖xe6   **♘xc5**
31.bxc5   **...**

Now, however, an advantage in this line of play is that 31...♖c8 to protect the black c-pawn is too passive. White can then play 32.♖e7+ and 33.♖a7, and if 33...♖f4 34.♖e2 winning Black's a-pawn.

31...   **♖f4**
32.♖1e2   **...**

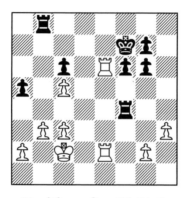

Position after 32.♖1e2

32...   **a4**

In view of the aforementioned note, Black tries to "mix it up" on the queenside.

33.♖xc6   **axb3**
34.axb3   **♖a8**
35.♔b2   **...**

White must stop the invasion on the seventh.

35...   **♖f1**

Black's plans are to double on the eighth rank and try to work up some mating threats. However, this is no compensation at all for the passed-pawn mass. White now takes defensive action to remove all threats.

36.b4   **...**

An escape hole.

36...   **♖8a1**
37.♔b3   **...**

The king will try to aid the passed pawns.

37... g5?

This shortens the game considerably. White now makes mating threats which force further simplification – now, of course, good for him.

38.♖c7+ ♔g6

Position after 38...♔g6

39.g4 ...

A typical Heisman move. The threat is 40.♖2e7, ♔h6 and then either rook to the eighth rank or ♖xg7.

39...	♖fe1
40.♖2e7	♖xe7
41.♖xe7	♖h1
42.c6	...

The quickest. Of course, 42.♖e3 also wins. Actually, I overlooked the fact that, after 42...♖xh3, 43...♖h8 is just in time to stop the queening.

42...	♖xh3
43.c7	♖h8
44.b5	f5
45.b6	1-0

Just as Black was about to establish material equality with 45...exg4 (tongue in cheek). Of course, on 45...♔f6, 46.b7 wins with plenty to spare.

Game 6

Did You See That 1600?

My first tournament of 1968 was not an especially good one. However, one high point, this game, became the basis for some "fame" in our small chess circle. In round 1 of this Swiss system event, I was now rated highly enough to find myself playing on Board 1 – this is to say, I was the top player *of all the lower-rated players*, the best of the second half, nothing more. Nevertheless, on this one occasion I was privileged enough to meet and beat the top-rated player, Master Sergei Goregliad, then the highest rated player in Philadelphia at 2242, causing at least one of the other players to comment to me later, "Say, did you see that 1600...?"

Dan Heisman (1676) – Sergei Goregliad (2242)
First Liberty Bell Open, Philadelphia 1968
Dutch Defense

1.d4   f5

What, Sergei doesn't allow me to play the Blackmar-Diemer Gambit, which I had been experimenting with at the time? Actually, Sergei chose this sharp opening against the much weaker player to complicate the game to his advantage. About fifteen moves later it looked as though his plan was working.

2.g3   ...

I had heard that this move was strong against the Dutch Defense, but that was about the extent of my book knowledge!

2...   g6
3.♗g2   ♘f6

Using the ultra-sharp Leningrad System of the Dutch is in accordance with the reasons stated on the notes after Black's first move.

4.c4   ♗g7
5.♘c3   0-0
6.♘h3   ...

To my utter amazement after the game, I found out that this move is "book" – and considered the best one, at that.

6...   **d6**
7.O-O   **...**

At this point, we depart the "book" (Bannik – Savon, USSR Championship 1963), which went 7.♘f4. I felt this line was bad for White because of 7...e5.

7...   **c6**

Plugging the thematic hole at d5.

8.♘g5(?)   **...**

Preparing e2-e4. However, this can be met by 8...h6 immediately.

8...   **e5(?)**
9.dxe5   **dxe5**
10.e4   **...**

This had to be calculated exactly because of Black's belated reply:

10...   **h6**

Although this drives away the knight, it creates a serious weakness in the kingside, soon to become fatal.

11.♘f3   **♕c7**

Black does not like the look of 11...fxe4 or 11...♘xe4 because his pawn structure is bad enough as it is. [*R*: good is 11...♕xd1 with equality, but who wants to trade queens this early with someone rated 600 points lower?]

12.♘h4   **...**

The fourth opening move of this knight is a strong one [*Rybka*: best!]. Now Black must allow the shattering of his kingside pawns.

12...   **♔h7**

[*R*: 12...♔h7 deserves a "?". Much better is 12...♕f7 with a nice edge to White.]

13.exf5   **gxf5**

Even more distasteful would be 12...♗xf5 13.♘xf5.

14.♕c2   **...**

Putting pressure on the hanging f-pawn.

14...   **e4**

Necessary, but this creates holes.

15.♗f4(?)   **...**

Up to now, White has played decently, but his play starts to crumble. Better was 15.♗h3 [*Rybka* says that even better is 15.f3! +−], putting more pressure on the black f-pawn. Although the text seems to develop with a tempo and blockade the pawns (which is why I chose it), the queen is actually driven to a better square and ♗g2-h3 is prevented.

15...   **♕f7**

Attacking the White c-pawn. Now 16.♗h3 can be met by 16...♘h5! and White is in trouble.

16.♖ad1?   **...**

White, harried by the occasion, does not realize he has left a pawn *en prise!* Black can safely take the pawn now. [Amazingly, at 15 ply *Rybka* rates 16.♖ad1 as best! I guess my intuition was very good that day! And my annotation later not so good...]

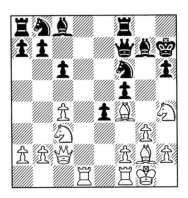

Position after 16.♖ad1?

16...   **♘a6(?)**

But Black decides to develop his queenside. The text has the threat of ...♘b4-d3 and keeps the threat on the c-pawn. When, after the game, I asked the post-mortem audience why Sergei didn't take my c-pawn, the situation was best summed up by one of Philadelphia's top players, the president of my Germantown Chess Club, Rich Pariseau: "When a 1600 player starts sacrificing pawns on you, you'd better be careful!" [R: 16... ♘a6 is best! If 16...♕xc4 17.b3! and White is winning, although there is a lot of chess to be played.]

17.♘e2 ...

To save the pawn and protect the f4-bishop after the knight lands on d3. [*Rybka* has a strong preference for 17.♗d6 with a winning position for White.]

17... ♘b4
18.♛b3 ...

The only square to protect the c- and a-pawns. White's poor queen is overworked. The white c-pawn is now pinned.

18... ♘d3

A fine square for the knight.

19.f3 ...

White must immediately begin to undermine the knight's position. The threat is 20.fxe4 fxe4 21.♗xe4+! ♘xe4 22.♛xd3.

19... ♗e6

Saves the pawn because of the overworked queen.

20.fxe4 ♗xc4
21.♛c2 ♘b4?

Black begins to falter. There seems nothing wrong with 21...fxe4 with great complications, though that could be why! One line might run 22.♗xe4+?! ♘xe4 23.♖xd3 ♗xd3 24.♛xd3 . [*R:* 21...♘b4 is no worse. If 21...fxe4 22.♗xh6! ♗xh6 23.♗xe4+ and in the complications White retains some advantage.]

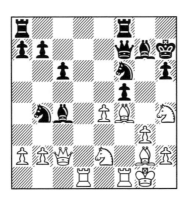

Position after 21...♘b4?

22.♛d2 ♖ad8

Black cannot take the a-pawn because of 23.♘xf5. [*Rybka* rates

22...fxe4 as best and leaves White with an edge after 23.♕xb4 ♗xe2 24.♗xe4+] It is important to note here that at this point I *felt* that I was being "rolled up," but actually I have a good game! The following few moves are forced.

23.♕xb4   ♗xe2
24.♖xd8   ♗xf1

The simple 24...♖xd8 was better. [*R:* wrong again. After 25.♖e1 White is doing at least as well as in the game.]

25.♖xf8   ♗xf8

Black must have foreseen this position and felt that it was a win. With his queen attacked, White seems to have no answer to 26...♗xg2 and 27...♘xe4 (or fxe4) with an easy win for Black.

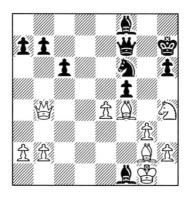

Position after 25...♗xf8

26.♕a5!   ...

White's only move – and *it* wins. White threatens 27.♗xf1 and 27.♕xf5+. Now, of course, 26...♗xg2 is answered by 27.♕xf5+, thus Black's reply...

26...   ♗b5
27.♘xf5   ♕c4

[*R:* 27...b6 is best, but after 28.♕c3 ♕xa2 29.h3 White still has excellent winning chances.]

28.♕c7+   ...

Black is still in trouble, but has plenty of aces up his sleeve. [*Rybka* has White winning easily.]

28...   ♔g8

Trappy and relatively best. If now 29.♘xh6+?? ♗xh6 30.♗xh6?? ♕d4+ 31. ♔h1 ♕d1+ 32. ♗f1 ♕xf1#. As long as the knight on f5 controls d4 and the bishop on g2 controls f1, Black has no threats. So, to release his pieces, White simply plays...

29.h3!   ...

The king will be perfectly safe on h2.

29...   ♕f7

He must come back to defend.

30.♘xh6+   ...

The crushing simplification.

30...   ♗xh6

Or else the queen goes.

31.♕xf7+   ♔xf7
32.♗xh6   ...

White has emerged from the fray with two extra pawns and the bishop-pair, surely enough to win; however, it looks as though his isolated e-pawn will fall. The way White saves it is instructive.

32...   ♗d3
33.e5   ♘d7
34.♗f4   ♔e6

Position after 34...♔e6

35.♗f1!   ...

A move I consider my finest of the game. Black cannot take the pawn without trading off both minor pieces, leaving White with a simple king-and-pawn endgame.

| 35... | ♗c2 |
| 36.♗c4+ | ♔f5 |

If 36...♔e7, then 37.♗g5+ and 38.e6 +– .

37.e6	♘f6
38.e7	♔g6
39.♗e5	...

Threatening 40.♗xf6.

| 39... | ♘e8 |
| 40.♔f2 | ... |

Black's king can't approach the passed e-pawn, so White's king will.

| 40... | b5 |
| 41.♗g8 | ... |

41.♗e6 might be quicker.

| 41... | c5 |

Trying to create a passed pawn.

| 42.h4 | ... |

Threatening 43.h5+, and if 43... ♔h5? then 44.♗f7+.

| 42... | ♗d1 |
| 43.♔e3 | ... |

To go to f4 and assist playing g3-g4.

| 43... | ♗h5 |

He must try to stop g3-g4.

| 44.♔f4 | ... |

Threatening the bishop.

| 44... | ♘f6 |

Allows 45.e8♕+ ♘xe8 46.g4 winning the bishop (suggested after the game by Philadelphia Expert Richard Lunenfeld, my opponent in Game 24), but White ends "elsewhere."

| 45.♗e6 | 1-0 |

Black cannot stop the threat of 46.g4, winning a piece. If 45...♔g7 46.g4 ♗e8 47.g5 and the unfortunate knight is lost.

Game 7

Pawn for – Bishop and Rook

My eventual college roommate, Ken Boehm, had his best tournament at the 1968 Philadelphia Championship; however, I dropped out with a 2-1 score to play in the Eastern States High School Championship. My only decent game from the three in the Philadelphia event was this "fine" positional defeat of Gil Raich, Germantown Chess Club's longest active U.S.Chess Federation member. After a terrible blunder in the opening, I was given a chance to right myself, but at the cost of a pawn. However, Mr. Raich had to use his bishop to protect the pawn for the rest of the game and he compounded his problems by making his rook a "living dead piece." What this all amounted to was victory for me because Mr. Raich had won a "pawn for – bishop and rook!"

Gil Raich (1750) – Dan Heisman (1670)
Philadelphia Open Championship 1968
Sicilian Defense

1.e4	c5
2.♘f3	d6
3.d4	cxd4
4.♘xd4	♘f6
5.♘c3	a6

My opponent can never be sure what I will play against him because sometimes I don't make up my mind until after the start of the game! This was, I believe, my first attempt at playing the Najdorf variation – the most popular master line. This was not my only bad experience with the Black side in this opening. Others were against Heinen at the U.S. Amateur 1968 and Frey at Bloomsburg 1968.

6.♗e2 ...

The tamest reply. 6.♗g5 is most popular and Fischer used to play 6.♗c4. Currently Ken Boehm plays 6.f4.

6... e6

I turn down a chance to follow the regular lines of the Boleslavsky

37

System, 6...e5, which Fischer would play. The game now transposes into a regular Scheveningen line.

7.f4 ...

White plays aggressively – and non-book. He will attempt to counter Black's queen bishop fianchetto with ♗f3.

7... **b5**

7...♗e7 and 8...O-O seem indicated, but Black wishes to gamble.

8.a3 ...

Over-cautious. Black has a hard time replying to 8.♗f3(!). If 8...♗b7 9.e5 seems good for White. On 8...♖a7, White can have his choice, with 9.O-O probably indicated.

8... **♗b7**
9.♗f3 **♗e7**

[*R:* inaccurate. Much better is 9...♘bd7 with almost equality. 9... ♗e7? allows 10.e5 ±.]

10.♗e3 ...

Why not 10.e5 ♗xf3 11.♕xf3 ? If instead 10...♘d5 11.♘xd5 ♗xd5 12.♗xd5 exd5 13.♘f5 ±.

10... **♘c6??**

After his series of blunders, Black finally finds one that loses by force. The queen's knight has never had any business on c6 in the Najdorf-type setup.

Position after 10...♘c6

11.e5 +− **♘d5**

Either this or lose a piece.

12.♘xd5   **♘xd4(!)**

On 12...exd5 White has his choice of excellent lines: 13.♗xd5, 13.♘f5, 13.exd6, etc.

13.♕xd4   **...**

On 13.♗xd4 exd5 14.exd6 ♗f6 Black may hold.

13...   **exd5**
14.exd6   **...**

If 14.♗xd5? dxe5 wins a piece for Black. [*R:* 14.O-O-O +−.]

14...   **♗f6**
15.♕b6??   **...**

Thank you. I was expecting 15.♕b4 holding the extra pawn on d6 and the white b-pawn. Now Black will get excellent chances to get back in the game.

15...   **♕xb6**
16.♗xb6   **♗xb2**
17.♖a2??   **...**

The losing move. The rook will never return into play. White may still keep the edge with 17.♖d1 ♗xa3 18.♗xd5 ♗b4+ 19.♔f2, for if 19...♗xd5 20. ♖xd5 ♔d7 21. ♖e1 ♖he8 ≈. White figures he will now win the d-pawn and win the game. He wins the d-pawn! [*R:* In the line above, Black is still somewhat better after 18...♗xd5 19.♖xd5 ♔d7.]

17...   **♗c3+**
18.♔f2   **♔d7**
19.♗c7   **...**

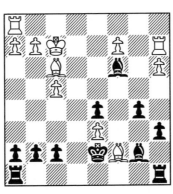

Position after 19.♗c7

Now Black ties up a bishop, too. This bishop's subsequent activity is negligible and the defended White d-pawn acts as a good shield for the black king!

19...   **g6!**

I thought a long time on this move. The idea is to be able to eventually answer ♗g4+ with ...f7-f5. Thus if 19...♖he8 20.♗g4+ ♚c6 21.d7. The immediate 19...f5 is not good because of 20.♖d1 and if 20...♚e6?? 21.♖e1+ and 22.♖e7 is strong. [*Rybka* assesses 19...♗d4+ as most accurate.]

20.♖d1   **♖he8(!)**

Black's idea – he can't keep the pawn, but he will activate his rooks, being essentially a rook up. Without ...g7-g6 White would now have 21.♗g4+ △ d6-d7 as in the previous note.

21.♗xd5   **♗xd5**
22.♖xd5   **♖e4**

Black activates his rooks with tempi.

23.♚f3   ...

White is understandably reluctant to further weaken himself with 23. g3.

23...   **♖ae8**
24.♖d3   ...

[*R:* Best is 24.♗b6, but even then Black has good winning chances.]

24...   **♖c4!**

To keep the rook trapped. Black's ensuing doubling of rooks along the fifth rank will eventually cause fatal weakenings in White's position. [According to *Rybka*, 24...♗d4 wins too and may be better, although it does finally allow the rook on a2 to escape.]

25.a4   ...

He wants out.

25...   **b4**

I want in.

26.a5   ...

This doesn't help, although I was scared for a moment that it might, since he played it so quickly.

| 26... | ♖8e4 |
| 27.g3 | ♖e1 |

[*R*: 27...♖cd4 is the most accurate, with a clear win for Black.] The threat is 28...♖4e4 and 29...♖4e2, so:

| 28.♖e3 | ♖xe3+ |
| 29.♔xe3 | ... |

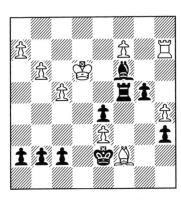

Position after 29.♔xe3

I'll gladly trade off a pawn down in the endgame – in this case. Black will have two active pieces to White's none.

| 29... | ♖d4 |

There is no stopping 30...♖d2.

| 30.h4 | ... |

Desperately trying to save his h-pawn.

| 30... | f5 |

Fixing Black's pawns as targets.

| 31.♔f3 | ♖d2 |
| 32.♔e3 | ♖g2(?) |

32...b3 immediately would win: 33.♖a3 b2 34.♖b3 (34.♖xc3 ♖d1! −+) 34...♖d1 −+ .

| 33.♔f3 | ♖h2 |
| 34.♔e3 | ... |

Hoping for a draw?

| 34... | b3 |

35.♖a3	b2
36.♖b3	♖h1
37.♔d3	...

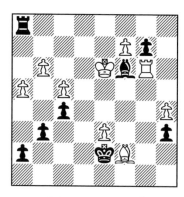

Position after 37.♔d3

| 37... | ♗f6 |

The last finesse. Black wins a whole rook and prevents ♖b8-d8+ with counterplay. The rest needs no comment.

38.c3	b1♕+
39.♖xb1	♖xb1
40.♔c4	♖c1
41.♔d5	♖xc3
42.♗b6	♖xg3
43.♔c5	♖c3+
44.♔d5	♖d3+
45.♔c4	♖xd6
46.♗c5	♖c6
47.♔d5	♗xh4
48.♗d4	♖d6+
49.♔c4	♗e1
50.♗b6	♖xb6
51.axb6	♔c6
0-1	

Game 8

Surprise!

Col. Ed Edmondson, USCF Executive Director, is well liked by all. At the 1968 U.S. Amateur I had occasion to meet him when I was paired with him for the 6th round. At this point, we both had 2½ points. I went on to win the "Under 18" prize at the tournament. Midway through this game my attack bogged down and I found myself in a seemingly hopeless position. After looking at the position for about 10 minutes and contemplating resigning, my jaw dropped – mentally. There was a saving move, so complicated and sacrificial that I couldn't believe it. After another 10 minutes' contemplation, I played my move and Edmondson took 35 of his remaining 40 minutes trying to refute it. He didn't, and it must have been as much of a surprise to him as it was to me when I made the original move.

Dan Heisman (1676) – Col. Ed Edmondson (1880)
U.S. Amateur, Philadelphia 1968
Sicilian Defense

1.e4	c5
2.♘f3	♘c6
3.d4	cxd4
4.♘xd4	d6

Inviting the Maróczy Bind.

5.♘c3	g6

No thanks. How about a Dragon?

6.♗e3	♗g7
7.♕d2	♘xd4

An old line. It avoids White's move ♗e3-h6.

8.♗xd4	♘f6
9.f3	...

White can just play 9.O-O-O, because the bishop no longer needs shielding, but figures an eventual kingside pawn storm needs f2-f3 to facilitate g2-g4. 9.f4 is also a good idea.

9...	O-O
10.O-O-O	b6(?)

A novelty (against me) and not a good one. The light squares on Black's queenside become weak and his queenside attack is slowed. Better is 10...♝e6 or 10...♛a5.

11.h4	...

White intends 12.h5 and 13.g4.

11...	♞h5?!
12.♝xg7	♚xg7

12...♞xg7? would be senseless because of 13.g4.

13.g4	♞g3
14.♜g1	...

Not 14.♜h3 ♞xf1 15.♜xf1 h6, and White cannot play 16.f4.

14...	♞xf1
15.♜dxf1	♝b7
16.h5	f6
17.g5	...

Open lines. The pawn is, of course, taboo. After 17...gxh5?? 18.gxf6+ ♚xf6 19.♛h6+ White wins at will.

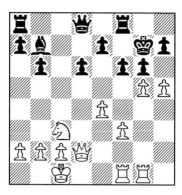

Position after 17.g5

17...	♛c8
18 gxf6+	...

18.f4 is certainly worth considering. [R: 18.♜e1! is the one worth considering, but 18.hxg6 hxg6 19.♜e1 is also good.]

18...	♖xf6
19.hxg6	hxg6
20.f4?!	...

20.♖h1 is much simpler and gives White much less trouble. Not forced by any means, but certainly interesting is the line 20.♖h1 ♛e8 21.♘d5 ♝xd5 22.exd5 ♛f8 23.♖e1 ♖xf3 24.♛h6+ ♚f6 25.♖e6+ ♚f5 26.♖h5+ gxh5 27.♛g6+ ♚f4 28.♖e4#.

20...	♛c4
21.f5?	...

[*R:* No question mark! This is best.]

21...	♝xe4
22.♖f4(?)	...

White continues to have delusions of grandeur. [*Rybka:* Yes, 22.♖f4 loses most of the advantage. White continues to roll after the correct 22.b3!.]

Position after 22.♖f4(?)

22...	d5

The continuation for which I had hoped. Immediately after I moved 22.♖f4, I realized 22...♛c5 was very strong, and to which I would have to reply 23.♖e1 ∓.

23.♖4g4	...

[White still has a nice advantage after the simple 23.♘xd4 or the more complex 23.♖xg6+, according to *Rybka*.]

23...	♖xf5

[Better is 23...♖c8.]

24.♖xg6+   ♔f7
25.♖g7+   ...

If 25.♕h6?? Black has at least 25...♖f1+ 26.♖xf1 ♕xf1+ 27.♘d1 ♗xg6 −+. [*R:* 25.b3! is the winning idea.]

25...   ♔e6
26.♖1g6+   ...

I disdain the endgame 26.♘xe4 ♖f1+ 27.♖xf1 ♕xf1+ 28.♕d1 ♕xd1+ 29.♔xd1 dxe4. [*R:* This move throws away most of White's advantage. Better is 26.♖e1 ±.]

26...   ♔d7
27.b3   ...

I had hoped this would help, but things just seemed to get worse:

27...   ♕f1+

[*R:* 27...♕b4! is almost equal.]

28.♔b2   ♖f2

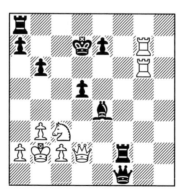

Position after 28...♖f2

Threatening my queen, my rook, and an eventual mate if my queen moves. e.g., 29.♕h6 ♖xc2+ 30.♔a3 ♗xg6 followed by a fatal dislocation of white pieces. At this point I desperately planned on 29.♘xe4 ♖xd2 30.♘xd2, which seemed the best I could hope for. All of a sudden I saw *it*; 10 minutes later...

29.♘xd5!!!   ...

Game 8: Surprise!

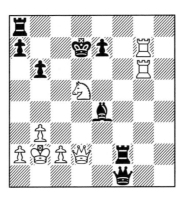

Position after 29.♘xd5!!!

Only good for a draw, but plenty of chances to win. Thirty-five minutes later came the Director's reply:

29... ♖af8?

The Colonel remarked that he now had hoped for 30.♘xb6+. ♔c7 31.♕d7+ ♔b8 and White has nothing. However, I announced mate in 6 and Edmondson resigned after the first move: **30.♖xe7+ (1-0)** 30... ♔d8 31.♖d6+ ♔c8 32.♕c3+ ♕c4 33.♕xc4+ ♔b8 34.♕c7+ ♔a8 35.♕xa7#.

Another win (after the game's 29...♖af8) is 30.♘xb6+ ♔c7 31.♕d6+ ♔b7 32.♖xe7+ ♔a6 33.♘c4+ ♔b5 34.a4 (or ♖e5) mate. Credit this line to Frank Gavlak, my best friend at Penn State.

The best line for Black is 29...♗xg6, which the Colonel said he would have tried if he had had more time. White then must play exactly to hold: 30.♘xb6+! ♔c6! 31.♖g6+ ♖f6 32.♘xa8 ♖xg6 33.♕c3+ and White has some chances: e.g., 33...♔b7? 34.♕c7+.

[Many years later when I got an Apple IIE, I used *Sargon III* to analyze this position. It came up with the following winning try for White: 29...♗xg6 30.♘xb6+ ♔c6 31.♖g6+ ♖f6 32.♘d5! ♖xg6 33.♘xe7+ ♔c7 34.♕c3+ △ 35.♘xg6 ±.]

[In 2010, running on a quad processor, in the line after 31...♖f6 *Rybka* suggests 32.♖g5 ♖d6 33.♘d5 (interesting is 33.♕a5!? ♕f6+ 34.♖e5! ♖ad8 35.♘c4 and White is likely winning) 33...♕f6+ 34.♔a3 e6 35.♘b4+ ♔d7 36.♕g2 ♖f8 37.♕b7+! ♔e8 38.♕b5+:

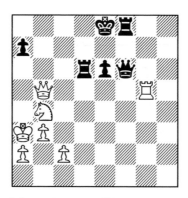

Position after 38.♕b5+ (analysis)

with good, but complex, winning chances.]

[It should be mentioned that, on his final move, Black cannot take the queen because of 29...♖xd2?? 30.♖xe7+ ♔d8 31.♖g8+ ♕f8 32.♖xf8#.]

Game 9

I Use Psychology

The 1968 Keystone State Tournament has been by far the best of my life. In what was to be a crucial game (I was 2-0 on my way to a 5-0 start in an open tournament where I was rated in the bottom half!), I met Rafael Cintrón in the third game. In these, his "younger" days, Mr. Cintrón favored a passive game, with a penchant for the endgame. He used to first trade queens, then rooks, bishops, and finally knights in that order. He has since changed his style in such a large manner that his favorite defense to e4 has changed from 1.e4 d6 2.d4 e5?! to 1.e4 e5 2.♘f3 d5?! – ! At the time, however, I was resolute to avoid the exchange of queens until it was to my great advantage. The result was a long, unusual, and most interesting game.

Rafael Cintrón (1920) – Dan Heisman (1716)
Keystone State Tournament, Philadelphia 1968
Sicilian Defense

| 1.e4 | c5 |
| 2.g3 | ... |

At the time, Cintrón's favorite variation versus the Sicilian. [Note: I think the next time I faced 2.g3 in a tournament game was 23 years later against my good friend Arthur Mitchell in the tournament where I gained my FIDE rating! I won that game, too.]

| 2... | e6 |

MCO-10 recommends 2...d5!. However, looking back (I didn't know of 2...d5), I'll bet Cintrón would have answered 3.d3?! and I would have played right into his hands!

3.d3	d5
4.♕e2	♘c6
5.c3	...

After 4.♕e2, this is probably necessary.

49

5...   ♘f6
6.♗g2   **...**

Later Cintrón said he wished he had played e4-e5 about this time.

6...   ♗e7

Black chooses the quiet path – so far.

7.f4   **...**

White aims for a sharp pawn duel.

7...   ♕c7

Black decides to accept a spatial advantage on the queenside.

8.♘a3(?)   **...**

Unnecessary. White can either play 8.♗e3 and 9.♘bd2, or the immediate 8.♘f3 and 9.0-0.

8...   **a6**

Black expands without loss of tempo.

9.♘f3   **b5**
10.0-0   ♗b7
11.h3(?)   **...**

White tries to prepare a kingside pawn roller. However, the text needlessly weakens the king's position, and since Black has not committed himself to kingside castling, he can exploit the weakened white g-pawn.

11...   **h5**

Logical and restricting. [*Rybka* prefers 11...c4! undermining the center.]

12.♗d2   **...**

White is showing signs of "crampedness." Black's pieces are better placed.

12...   **c4**

Now Black sharpens the struggle. Here is where psychology comes into play. The main purpose of this move was to "threaten" 13...♗xa3 which, due to Cintrón's love of knights, would be more advantageous to me than just harming White's pawn structure.

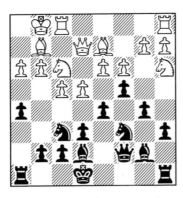

Position after 12...c4

Faced with such a "threat," White now makes the decisive blunder.

13.dxc4??   ♘xe4

Of course. The threat of 14...♘xg3 winning the exchange enables Black to win a pawn, trade bishop for knight, and ruin White's pawn structure. Black's advantage is now decisive. However, the rest is instructive as I play what was probably my best ending against an experienced endgame player. Just to make it interesting, I did make one ghastly oversight on move 32.

14.♗e1   ♗xa3
15.bxa3   bxc4
16. ♕e3?   ...

This is a bad square for the queen, as will be seen. [*Rybka:* Better are 16.♘g5 or 16.♖b1 when White has chances to survive.]

16...   ♘e7(!)

Black now threatens ...♘f5 and/or ...♕c5.

17.♘h4?   ...

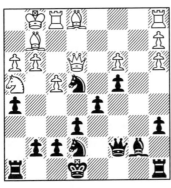

Position after 17.♘h4

He stops 17...♘f5 but allows the exchange of queens, facilitating Black's task. Compare how the board looks when White plays his knight to h4 and how it looks (on move 45!) when it is finally taken off h4!

17...   **♛c5**

Now I trade queens.

18.♛xc5   **♘xc5**

The knight heads for the even more advantageous outpost at d3.

19.♗f2   **♘d3**
20.♗d4   **...**

White uses the only resources he has at his disposal: The bishop-pair, control of the central black squares, and *temporary* control of the b-file.

20...   **f6**

Black plugs some holes.

21.♖ab1   **♗c6**
22.♖b6   **♔d7**
23.♖fb1   **...**

Contains a hidden threat.

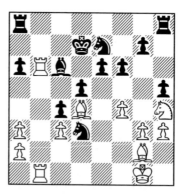

Position after 23.♖fb1

23...   **♔c7!**

If Black plays to win the exchange with 23...♘c8, he probably loses the game, e.g., 24.♖b7+! ♗xb7 25.♖xb7+ ♔d6 26.♖xg7 and the white knight and queen's bishop enter the game with strong effect. Now, however, Black threatens 24...♘c8 with no complications, so White must clear a square with his rook, thus allowing Black to obtain a stranglehold on the b-file, allowing him to simplify further. However, the process is a delicate one.

24.♖d1	♖hb8
25.♖xb8	♖xb8
26.♗f1	...

He tries to rid himself of the well-positioned knight.

26...	♗a4

The formerly dormant bishop becomes active.

27.♖d2	...

27.♖xd3 is no help at all.

27...	♖b2
28.♖xb2	♘xb2
29.♗e2	...

White now tries to activate his pieces.

29...	♗d1 ∓

The only move and the key one involved in the combination starting with 26...♗a4.

30.♗f1	...

If 30.♗xd1 ♘xd1 followed by 31...♘c6 wins quickly.

30...	♘a4

Black threatens 31...♘c6 with immediate decisiveness. There is no defense.

31.♔f2	♘c6
32.♔e1	...

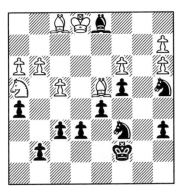

Position after 32.♔e1

53

32...   e5?

Black delays the game for 15 moves. Of course, after 32...♘xd4 there is no answer: e.g., 33.♔xd1 ♘xc3+ 34.♔c1 (34.♔e2 ♘xa2 and ...c3-c2-c1♛) 34...♘(either)e2+ *finis.* Or 33.cxd4 ♗c2 △ ...♗b1 and then ...♗xa2 or ...c3-c2.

33.fxe5   fxe5
34.♗e3   ♗c2
35.♔d2   ♗e4

Winning the a-pawn does not speed matters. Black now had to search hard for the correct way to make headway.

36.♗g5   ♘b2
37.♗e2   g6
38.♔e3   ♔d6

Originally made as a "nothing" move, this advance of the king to the kingside is the correct procedure.

39.♗h6   ♔e6
40.♗f8   ♘e7

Back on the right track. 41...♘f5+ is a winning threat.

41.g4   hxg4
42.♗xg4+   ♘f5+

White's check is answered by a winning check.

43.♔d2   ♔f7!

The finish. By moving out of the pin Black forces another large-scale simplification.

44.♗xf5   ...

Forced. If 44.♘xf4, then 44...gxf4 wins a piece.

44...   ♗xf5(!)
45.♘xf5   ...

Either this or White loses yet another pawn.

45...   gxf5

Of course. But oddly enough, it took me about ten minutes to realize that the bishop is absolutely useless in the ensuing endgame.

46.♗c5   f4
47.♗d6   ♘d3
48.♔e2   e4

White can do nothing against the pawn advance.

49.♗c7　　　　　　**♔g6**

The king will assist the advance of the pawns and, if needed, can win the h-pawn.

50.♗d8　　　　　　**♔h4**
51.h4　　　　　　...

This facilitates Black's plan. But if 51.♗e7 ♘e5 and the maneuver ...♘f3-g5 is one possibility for an easy win.

51...　　　　　　**♔g4**
52.♗f6　　　　　　**e3**
0-1

He does not care for 53...♘c1+ and 54...f3.

Game 10

My Best Game

A fter defeating R. Cintrón in a positional struggle in the previous round (see Game 9), my perfect 3-0 score was matched only by John Yehl's identical 3-0 mark. It was obvious that we would be paired – and ironic, for a few rounds before I had promised Yehl that we would meet again. In our previous encounter, Yehl thought 45 minutes on his 13th(?) move in a hopeless position. Soon thereafter *I* fell into a mate in one, missing a chance to go into the endgame two pieces to the good! What resulted in our second encounter was an exciting, tactical slugfest with such unfathomable complications that more than a year of analysis has been put into the game with no definite answers. So far, no improvement has been found in Black's play. Players from Aki Kanamori (then Caltech's best player, now a British master) on East have assisted in annotations. *Chess Review* turned down an appeal from me to have the game annotated (not published!). Admittedly, as I sit down to relate the game to you, I am attempting the most difficult task I have tried at this game. By definition, my analysis will have omissions, but I will do my best to relate the struggle.

John Yehl (1951) – Dan Heisman (1716)
Keystone State Tournament, Philadelphia 1968
Sicilian Defense

| 1.e4 | c5 |
| 2.d4 | ... |

The Morra Gambit. In a later tournament, I saw Yehl reply 2. ♘f3 and inquired why he had not done so against me in the present game. He replied that he felt that I was "booked up" and that he had a better chance to win by taking me out of the book. Strangely enough, I was not booked up at all for this tournament (occurring on the July 4 holiday, right after school) and, of course, his strategy failed miserably.

| 2... | e6 |

A spur-of-the-moment decision. As I have previously noted, one cannot tell what I will play over the board in an opening because sometimes I don't even know myself. I believe I was trying to steer into a French or a Benoni after 3.d5, the latter a policy which has served me rather poorly (½-1½).

3.♘f3   ...

White opts for a Sicilian. Having declined the Morra, Black does not wish to change course with 3...cxd4, which is objectively best. My alternative can be considered my only questionable move of the game because it supposedly leads into a poor line for Black.

3...   **d5**

The Marshall Variation, supposedly weak because Black prematurely opens up his game and saddles himself with an isolated d-pawn. However, Botvinnik has had success with an isolated d-pawn because it affords free development and an open, tactical game. *MCO-10* gives 4.exd5 exd5 5.♗b5+ ♘c6 6.0-0 ♘f6 7.♘e5 ♗d7 8.♗xc6 bxc6 9.♖e1 ♗e7 10.dxc5 0-0 11.♗g5 ± Keres-Konstantinopolsky, USSR Championship 1950.

4.dxc5   ...

White chooses to isolate the pawn immediately.

4...   **♗xc5**
5.exd5   **exd5**

Of course not 5...♕xd5 6.♕xd5 (or 6.♗b5+) and the isolated d-pawn becomes an endgame liability.

6.♗b5+   **♘c6**

I thought for a long time on this move. 6...♗d7 7.♕xd5 ♗xb5 8.♕xc5 does not seem sound for Black and 6...♘d7 is obviously worse.

7.0-0   **♘e7**

Very necessary. On 7...♘f6, 8.♖e1+ becomes embarrassing and the pin with development ♗c1-g5 is very strong for White.

8.♘c3(?)   ...

The text is poor. The knight belongs on d2 after the development of the queen's bishop. It also should protect the king's knight, which will be pinned to the queen by Black's next move, ...♗c8-g4.

8...   **♗g4**
9.♖e1   ...

White now threatens the d-pawn by simply 10.♕xd5 or 10.♘xd5.

9...   **O-O**

Unpinning the knight protects the d-pawn. 9...d4 10.♘e4 is very strong for White and the d-pawn becomes fatally weak.

10.♗d3?   **...**

The beginning of trouble. White moves the bishop a second time before completing his development. His threat is now 11.♗xh7+ ♔xh7 12.♘g5+ regaining the piece with a pawn and interest.

10...   **f5(!)**

The text looks risky. First of all, I had to check the game continuation. Black's weakening of his kingside and some of the central squares is overcome by his gain of space, command of e4, and refutation of the threat mentioned in the previous note.

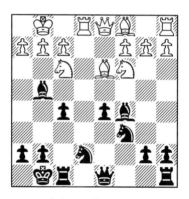

Position after 10...f5

11.h3?   **...**

The beginning of a faulty plan. White plans to kick the bishop by sacrificing his h- and g-pawns for Black's f-pawn, then "saccing" the bishop at h7 to regain it: i.e., 11...♗h5 12.g4 fxg4 13.hxg4 ♗xg4 14.♗xh7+ ♔xh7 15.♘g5+ ♔-any 16.♕xg4. But I had seen further.

11...   **♗h4**
12.g4? −+   **...**

White continues with this faulty plan. Better is simply 12.♗g5.

12...   **fxg4**
13.hxg4(?)   **...**

White still does not know what is coming. After the game 13.♘g5 was analyzed, but to no avail. Black can simply get away with 13...♗xf2+ and 14...♗xe1 and White does not have enough for the exchange.

13...   **♗xg4**

The only way to fly. Suddenly it all dawns on White and he consumes about 25 minutes on his next move, which is easily seen to be forced. He has now used up approximately an hour [most tournaments in those days were about 48 moves in 2 hours, so White had less than an hour for the next 34 moves].

14.♗e2 □   **...**

Of course! White overlooked 14.♗xh7+ ♔h8! and wins. White would then have no way of protecting his knight on f3, a consequence of putting his other knight on c3 and, of course, moving his g-pawn. Now Black has an easy win. He is a pawn up with a better position and a far safer king. A simple win is obtained by maneuvering the queen to the kingside via d6 or e8, a plan I might adopt today. [Note: Many years later, I fed the position into the computer, which is quite good at this sort of tactical play and, after the black queen reaches g6, White cannot hold out for very long. Some of the lines are quite beautiful, but really irrelevant to the discussion of how the game was actually played.] However, as mentioned in the introduction to this game, I was out for revenge in a big way – and I try to make the game exciting – so I play what turns out to be one of the finest conceptual attacks I have ever seen, if I do say so myself. The rest of the game is a super-abundance of tactical possibilities which have left me baffled. Most of the lines I will present were not found over the board because I frankly didn't have enough time. Yet they are still there, and it all begins with:

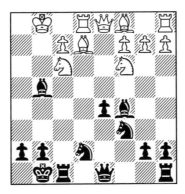

Position after 14.♗e2

14...   **♗xf2+!!**

The fun begins. White, of course, cannot refuse the sacrifice and has nothing to lose by accepting it, so he plays...

15.♔xf2   **♘e5**

Before 14...♗xf2+, I thought that 15...♘e5 would win back my piece immediately. Then, to my horror, I discovered the move 16.♗g5! with great complications, and the obvious lines turn out good for White when he sacrifices his queen, as will be seen! About 15 minutes later, to my dismay (and later joy because of the eventual complications), Mr. Yehl played...

16.♗g5!   **...**

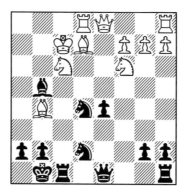

Position after 16.♗g5!

The only move and a good one. Now it was my turn to think and I did so for over half an hour, going over the one-hour mark. I wished that the time control was 16/2½! It seemed that I could study the position for hours on end and not come to a definite conclusion. One year later I can postulate that I was correct. In the other room friends Jerry Kolker and Lester Shelton were analyzing the position and, with moving the pieces(!), were having trouble comparing the relative merits of 16...♘xf3 and 16...♗xf3. I do not remember which one championed which move. The relative drawbacks of each are illustrated by the main variation of the position: 16...♘xf3 (or 16...♗xf3) 17.♗xf3! ♖xf3+ 18.♕xf3! ♗xf3 (or 18...♘xf3) 19.♗xe7 followed by ♔xf3. The resultant position is unclear. White has an exposed king, with rook, knight, and bishop for a queen and two connected passed pawns. I feel White should hold. However, this is only the main variation. At different points Black can interpose the check ...♕d8-b6+ and may manage to improve on the line. However, due to lack of space and the fascinating complexity of the position, I will leave it up to future generations to find the best lines after 16...♘xf3 or 16...♗xf3. My move is more clearcut, although I didn't fully comprehend my plan at the time. Growing disgusted with the complications, I disgustedly played:

**16...				♕b6+!!**

Now my knight is hanging. If White plays 17.♔f1, I leave my knight hanging with 17... ♗h3#. On 17.♔g2, things are unclear, but 17...♘xf3 looks winning:

A) 18.♗xf3? ♗xf3+ 19.♕xf3 ♖xf3 20.♔xf3 ♖f8+ 21.♔g4 (or else ...♕f2+) and Black has a simple win, having both an extra piece and a bigger attack than in the main line mentioned earlier after an immediate capture on f3.

B) 18.♗xe7 ♘xe1+ with unclear complications. Perhaps 18...♕g6?!? is better: 19.♕xd5+ ♔h8 20.♗xf8 ♖xf8 with a strong attack.

17...♗xf3 also looks unclear but is maybe more forcing. [Note: I recently fed the position after 17.♔g2 into John Stanback's fine program, *Zarkov 3*, and the only move it would consider playing for Black was 17...♖xf3, with the idea of just winning a piece and, after 18.♖f1, simply playing 18...♖xf1 19.♕xf1 ♕xb2 and Black is up three pawns; *Zarkov 3* also basically confirmed that all the rest of my moves in this game are correct, with the exception being on the final two moves when White could have resigned anyway!] Perhaps if then White had decided upon 17.♔g2, Black would have been better off trying this 17...♗xf3, though in great time trouble he may not have been able to navigate in troubled seas. Not willing to give back the piece, White has only one reply left and it appears to be the most forcing. However, the drawbacks will still be apparent.

**17.♗e3				...**

I had originally intended to answer the text with 17...♕e6, holding the d-pawn and probably regaining the piece on f3. However, it soon became apparent to me that I had a stronger, more forcing continuation.

**17...				♕f6**

For all intents and purposes, this is the move that ends the struggle. Black threatens 18...♕h4+, which must be stopped, explaining White's reply. However, if White does allow Black to penetrate on the kingside, very beautiful lines occur. For instance, if White plays 18.♘xd5?, then 18...♕h4+ and:

A) 19.♔f1? ♗h3+ 20.♔g1 ♕g3+ 21.♔h1 ♕g2#.

B) 19.♔g2 ♕h3+ 20.♔f2 (20.♔g1 transposes into line C below) 20... ♕h2+ 21.♔f1 ♗h3#.

C) 19.♔g1 ♕g3+ 20.♔h1 (20.♔f1? ♗h3#) 20...♗xf3+! 21.♗xf3:

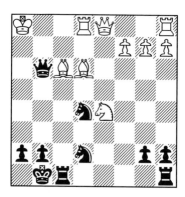

Position after 21.♗f3 (analysis)

21...♘xf3! 22.♘xe7+ ♔h8 and White must play 23.♕xf3+ to stop mate. (23.♖e2 ♕h3+ mates.) Admittedly, I did not see this line over the board, and it is undoubtedly one of the prettiest lines in this book.

18.♖h1   **...**

This move appears to be best, because White must give back a piece. However, it allows a nice finish. Other moves are also inadequate:

A) 18.♖g1 (to prevent the continuation actually played in the game.) 18...♕h4+ 19.♖g3 (19.♔g2 ♗h3+ 20.♔h1 {20.♔h2 ♘xf3+ mates} 20... ♘xf3 and wins) 19...♘xf3 and White is helpless, e.g., 20.♗xf3 ♖xf3+ 21.♕xf3 ♗xf3 is hopeless for White.

B) 18.♔g2 ♘xf3 (among others). Now this line is much stronger than it was two(!) moves ago with the white bishop on g5. Black's other knight is not attacked and Black threatens ...♘xe1+.

C) 18.♔g3 ♘f5+ 19.♔f2 ♘xe3 20.♔xe3 ♕f4+ 21.♔f2 ♗xf3 22.♗xf3 ♘g4+!? 23.♔g1? (but 23.♔f1 ♕xf3+ with a winning game for Black) 23... ♕g3+ 24.♗g2 ♕h2#. Black has many finesses in this line: 21...d4! or 22... ♕h2+ winning the Queen for a Rook. Black has no troubles with 18.♔g3.

D) 18.♔g1 or 18.♔f1 – Here Black can simply win back his piece with 18...♗xf3, opening the g-file with a continued decisive attack. The white king no longer protects the knight, so Black has no worries. Also, on

18.♔f1, Black stays in the pin and on 18.♔g1, he is on the vulnerable g-file after 18...♗xf3.

White's busted.

18...   **♗xf3**

At last! Black will win back his piece.

19.♗xf3   **♘g4+**

Or will he?! I could have played 19...♗xf3, but I wanted to be dastardly. In addition, the text is stronger and prettier, not to mention more forcing. White's queen appears to be lost.

20.♔e1   **...**

A) 20.♔g1 leads to a line similar to the game: 20...♘xe3 21.♗xd5+ (he can hold out longer by giving up another piece with, say, 21.♕e2) 21...♘7xd5 (if White played 21.♘xd5 then 21...♕g5+ wins the queen) and White has no moves.

B) 20.♔g3 leads to the last cute lines: 20...♘f5+!:

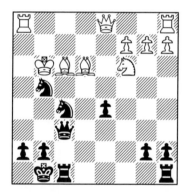

Position after 20...♘f5+! (analysis)

(during the game I saw this possibility, but had contemplated playing the simpler 20... ♘xe3; however, if Yehl had played 20.♔g3, I might have looked further into 20...♘f5+! and played it; one will never know) 21.♔h3 ♕h4+ 22.♔g2 ♘5xe3+ 23.♔g1 ♕f2#. This last line has just occurred to me – interestingly, no one has ever pointed out this obvious continuation! Previously, my analysis had continued 22...♕g3+ 23.♔f1 ♘(either)xe3+ –+ .

Now, finally, I do win back my piece – with interest.

20...   **♘xe3**
21.♘xd5   **...**

To answer 21...♘xd1 with 22.♘xf6+.

21...	**♘7xd5**
22.♗xd5+	**♚h8**

I took a while to play this. I wanted to make sure 23.♖xh7+ did not work. I did not wish to get swindled from my brilliancy. Of course 23.♖xh7+ ♚xh7 24.♕h5+ ♕h6 wins a rook for Black.

23.♕d2 ...

Objectively best. (Subjectively best is resigns.) White must stop 23... ♕f2#.

23...	**♘xd5**
24.♕xd5	...

"Better" is 24.c3, to answer 24...♖ae8+ 25.♚d1 ♕f3+ with 26.♚c2, although 26...♖e2 is strong. Note that White cannot castle queenside because he has moved his king (7.O-O; also 15.♚xf2, 20.♚e1) although both his king and king's rook have returned to their original positions! – just kidding a little.

Position after 24.♕xd5

24...	**♕f2+**
25.♚d1	**♖ad8**
0-1	

He might be able to avoid the loss of a whole queen. Not 26.♕xd8+ ♖xd8+ 27.♚c1 ♕d2+ 28.♚b1 ♕d1+ 29.♖xd1 ♖xd1#. This would have been a fitting finish. However, "better" is 26.c4 when 26...♖xd5+ 27.cxd5 ♕f3+ 28.♚c2 ♖c8+ 29.♚d2 ♕xd5+ will probably mate, e.g., 30.♚e3 ♖e8+ 31.♚f4 ♖e4+ 32.♚g3 ♕d3+ 33.♚g2 ♖e2+ 34.♚g1 ♕g3+ 35.♚f1 ♕f2#.

Finally – *finis*.

Game 11

Morra Lessa

As the tournament trail winds and one occasionally dabbles in the Sicilian Defense, he will periodically (as was the case in Game 10, also) come across the Morra Gambit, a pawn sacrifice played by those hardy souls who do not wish to get caught in one of the myriad book lines of the Sicilian. One of the strongest of this breed among the players I have come across is G. F. Miller, who was 5-0 going into the last round of the U.S. Amateur last year. However, to be prepared against the Morra is a distinct advantage and, although I missed the best continuation in the opening, I still obtained an easy equality. That's all I ever want as Black!

G.F. Miller (2000) – Dan Heisman (1926)
Merrimac Grand Prix, New Hampshire 1968
Sicilian Defense

1.e4	**c5**
2.d4	**cxd4**
3.c3	**♘f6**

Chess Digest Editor Ken Smith says this is a no-no, but we shall find out (maybe) when the Feb. 1970 *Chess Digest* is out.

4.e5	**♘d5**
5.♗c4(?)	**...**

5.cxd4 would seem more natural. Of 5.♗c4 the eminent theoretician Jerry Kolker (a very fine opening expert in Philadelphia in the 1960s) says, "This loses by force." I doubt it, but nevertheless, it is not best.

5...	**♘b6**

This natural move is not the strongest. Book and better is 5...♕c7(!).

6.♗b3	**...**

Perhaps 6.♗d3 is to be considered with White contemplating a kingside attack.

6...	**d5(!)**

Black wishes for a reversed French with his queen's bishop liberated. More typical of this declined line was 6...d6, which I rejected because of 7.e6?!, certainly a Miller-type move. To 7.e6 Kolker simply suggests

7...&xe6 "and wins," but after 8.&xe6 fxe6 Black may have slight difficulties developing and must watch for his king's safety. After the text he should have no trouble.

7.cxd4   ...

After 7.exd6 Black can play the "thematic" 7...e6 followed by 8... &xe6 with good prospects, or simply 7...♕xd6, which would run similar to the line in *MCO-10*.

7...   **&f5**
8.♘c3   **♘c6**
9.♘1e2   ...

Wishing to undermine the position of Black's strong bishop.

9...   **♖c8**
10.h4?!   ...

This move is weak. However, Black must be careful and I took a long time deciding upon my next move.

10...   **h6**

Best. I finally rejected 10...h5 because then the g5 square would become weak and I was not strong on the black squares. Also, my kingside pawn structure would be weakened after 11.♘g3 &g6 just as White's kingside is eventually weak.

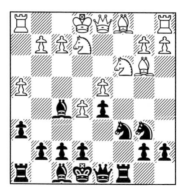

Position after 10...h6

11.&f4(?)   ...

White's 11th move seems weak and after this move I grew confident. However, the alternatives are not much better:

A) 11.O-O e6.

B) 11.♘g3 [best and equal, according to *Rybka*] 11...♗h7 12.O-O e6.

C) 11.♗e3 e6 followed by 12...♘a5 or 12...a6.

11...	e6
12.a3(?)	...

White is wary of 12...♘b4 and 13...♘d3, but he weakens his queenside. Unfortunately for White, after 12.O-O ♗e7 is dangerous, for if 13.h5 then 13...♗g4.

12...	♗e7

[*R:* 12...♘c4! and Black is much better.]

13. ♗g3	...

Sad; this saddles two pieces to the defense of a pawn, but 13.g3 would seriously weaken the kingside and cut down on the mobility of the king's knight. [*R:* best is 13.♘g3.]

13...	a6

Black wants first to prevent all possibility of ♘b5-d6 before he undertakes any offensive. With the closed center he can rightly delay capturing.

14.♗c2	...

Faced with the threat of 14...♘a5, White decides to trade off Black's pesky bishop.

14...	♗xc2
15.♕xc2	♘c4

A square! Black now threatens to overrun the queenside with ...b7-b5, ...♕d8-b6, and pressure on the d-pawn.

16. b4(?)	...

It looks bad to create such an outpost for the knight, especially one that cannot be easily traded off. Of course, 16.b3? ♘xa3 and 17.O-O? ♗xh4 sorely restricted White's constructive moves.

16...	b5

Black now dominates. He threatens ...♕d8-b6 and/or ...a6-a5. White is in trouble.

17.♕d3	...

Allows a combination, but what else can be done?

17...	♘xa3!

[*R:* A better move order is 17...O-O 18.♗f4 ♘xa3!.]

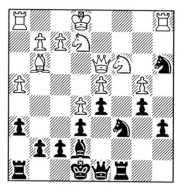

Position after 17...♞xa3!

The first of three fairly nice combinations in this game. Black wins material and ensures a won endgame. Less spectacular but just as sure was 17...♛b6, although the purpose of White's last move was to let him castle after 17...♛b6.

18.♖xa3	**♞xb4**
19.♛b1	**♞c2+**
20.♛xc2	**♝xa3**
21.O-O	**♝e7!**

Black could not play 21...b4? because of 22.♛a4+ and ♛xa6 and the bishop on a3 eventually hangs if Black takes on c3.

22.♛a2(!) ...

The only move against the threats of 22...♝xh4 and 22...b4; after 22...b4 23.♛a4+ ♛d7 24.♛xd7 ♚xd7 with an easy endgame.

22...	**♛b6**
23.♖b1	...

Position after 23.♖b1

With hopes of playing an eventual ♘c3-a4, which is impossible now because of the answer ... ♕a5.

23...   **♔d7**

A difficult decision – I decided the king was safer in the center, although I now allow 24.♘a4, e.g., 24...♕a5?? 25.♘c5+ winning the queen. However, I could meet 24.♘h4 with 24...♕a7.

[*R:* 23...♔d7? 24.♘xd5 exd5 25.♕xd5+ ♔e8 26. ♕f3 ♖c4 and Black has very little advantage. Best was 23....O-O.]

24.f4??   **♖c4(?)**

Obsessed with my plan, I miss the obvious 24...♖xc3 25.♘xc3 ♕xd4+ 26.♗f2 ♕xc3, with which, after 27.♕xa6, I am probably better off than following the game continuation, although *the game continuation is safer and probably easier on* Black.

25.♗f2   **♕c6**
26.♖b3   **...**

If 26.♗e1, then 26...b4 and 27...♖c2 is very strong.

26...   **♖c8**
27.♗e1   **...**

Again directed against ...b5-b4.

27...   **♔e8!**

A necessary preliminary to ...b5-b4, as will be seen. [*R:* Wrong! The immediate 27...b4! was best.]

28.♔h2   **...**

White is helpless against the ensuing simplifying combination which either nets Black a piece or else takes him into the endgame up a rook for a piece with a pawn to boot. The longest variation is the game continuation. [*R:* 28.♕b1 puts up the most resistance.]

28...   **b4**
29.♘a4   **...**

Best. If 29.♘b1/d1, then 29...♖c2 30.♖b2 ♖xb2 31.♕xb2 ♕c2 yields Black a quick endgame, as White will soon have to sacrifice a piece for a passed pawn, e.g., 32.♕xc2 ♖xc2 33.♘g3 ♖c1.

29...   **♖c2**

Now the reason for 27...♔e8 becomes apparent; White could otherwise now play 30.♘c5+ and win the exchange.

30.♖b2   ...

Obviously forced.

30...   ♕**c4!**

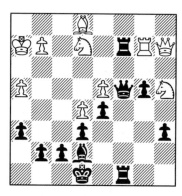

Position after 30...♕c4!

The key to the combination. White cannot avoid a disaster. There is nothing to be done against the threat of 31...♕xa2, e.g., 31.♖xc2 ♕xc2 32.♕xc2 ♖xc2 with 33...b4-b3; or White could play 32.♘4c3 when Black could transpose into the game continuation.

31.♘2c3   ...

Desperate but doomed.

31...   ♕**xa2**

Simple and deadly.

32.♖xa2   ...

If 32.♘xa2 ♖xb2 33.♘xb2 ♖c2 34.♘xb4 ♗xb4 35.♗xb4 ♖xb2.

32...   ♖**xa2**
33.♘xa2   ♖**c2**

The powerful rook...

34.♘xb4   ♗**xb4**
35.♗xb4   ♖**c4**

...wins in all variations!

36.♘c5   ♖**xb4**
37.♘xa6   ♖**xd4**
38.♔g3   ♔**d7**

39.♔f3   **♔c6**

The knight has been trapped – the final combination.

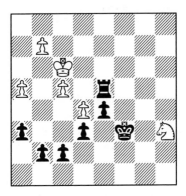

Position after 39...♔c6

40.♘b8+	**♔c7**
41.♘a6+	**♔b7**
42.♘c5+	**♔c6**
43.♘a6	**...**

If instead 43.♘b3, then 43...♖d3+.

43...   **♖a4**

On 44.♘b8+, 44...♔c7 quiets White.

0-1

Game 12

"Positional Patience"

Admittedly, this game is not spectacular, but it does indicate the maturing outlook of a young chessplayer. It is well known that only after much experience does a younger player pick up the patience and understanding to play a positional battle: maneuvering, squares, etc. In this game, White takes the minimal advantage afforded him in a familiar opening, sits on his advantage and, admittedly with the aid of his opponent, quietly announces the mate. Positional maturity or lack of ideas? – judge for yourself.

Dan Heisman (1700) – Gerald Johnson (1700)
Germantown Invitational, Philadelphia 1968
Sicilian Defense

1.e4	c5
2.♘f3	♘c6
3.d4	cxd4
4.♘xd4	♘f6
5.♘c3	e6
6.♘db5	...

According to the latest edition of *Shakhmatny Byulleten*, this variation can be considered satisfactory for Black and White should look for more in, say, changing White's 7th move from a2-a3 to ♗c1-f4. But the follow-up to White's 7th move leaves him with certain positional advantages to be discussed later.

6...	♗b4
7.a3	♗xc3
8.♘xc3	d5
9. cxd5	exd5

9...♘xd5 is an alternative.

10.♗d3	O-O

In the recent tournament in San Juan where Walter Browne gained his International Grandmaster title, he played 10...d4 [a popular move in this line 42 years later] as Black, to which his opponent replied with the inferior 11.♘e2. 11.♘e4 is better.

11.O-O

Now let us look at White's advantages:

A) His pawn structure is better.

B) He has the two bishops.

Admittedly, this is usually not enough to win, but it is a good psychological advantage in that Black has to avoid the endgame if at all possible.

11...	**♗g4**
12.f3	**♗h5**
13.♔h1	**...**

I prefer to get my king into immediate safety without having to worry about bothersome queen checks. My opponent had been in this position before, but he told me that his opponent had delayed playing ♔g1-h1. [*Rybka* prefers the immediate 13.♗g5 with some advantage.]

| **13...** | **h6** |

Black fears the pin ♗c1-g5, but weakens his kingside. The lack of a black bishop is hurting him already. [*Rybka* rates 13...d4 as best.]

| **14.♖e1** | **...** |

Position after 14.♖e1

| **14...** | **♘e7** |

Black probably did not like 14...♖e8 15. b4 or just 15. ♗f4. [*R:* this is where Black starts to get into trouble. Again much better is 14...d4.]

| **15.b4** | **...** |

White abandons the good diagonal for his queen's bishop and chooses a better one. The drawback here is that White's c-pawn could well become backward on the semi-open c-file.

15...   **♗g6**

It is understandable that Black would want to rid White of the bishop pair. However, he is losing time by moving his bishop so many times. This is acceptable in a closed game, but this one is far from closed!

16.♗b2   **♗xd3**
17.♕xd3   **♖e8**
18.♖ad1   **♕b6**

The text can be considered questionable. Alternatives are 18...♖c8 and 18...♕c7. Not 18...♘g6 because of 19.♖xe8+ and 20.♘xd5.

19.♘a4   **...**

White seizes the chance to occupy c5 without loss of tempo.

19...   **♕d6**

Black misses White's reply.

20.c4   **...**

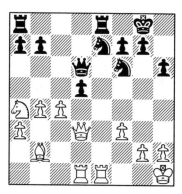

Position after 20.c4

White rids himself of his only weakness. [*R:* Much better was 20.♗e5 with a nice advantage to White.]

20...   **♖ad8**

[Missing the necessary 20...♕c6!.]

21.c5   **...**

White cedes a central passed pawn to Black to get an outside queenside majority – another positional advantage for the endgame.

21...   ♕d7

Black is becoming pressed for space. Unfortunately, his queen abandons the knight on the kingside and White gets a chance to open up the black king. However, if 21...♕c6 22.b5 so there was nothing to be done: 21...♕f4 and White has the pleasant choice of:

* Doubling rooks;

* Playing ♗e5-d6; or

* g2-g3 with an eventual ♗xf6.

22.♗xf6   **gxf6**

White's positional booty increases: Black has an exposed king and a wretched pawn structure. Luckily for Black, a knight on g6 usually is strong with this structure – if it weren't for the weak pawn on h6 instead of h7.

23.♘c3   ...

White's knight begins a remarkable tour that ends up with the knight assisting in a mating combination.

23...   ♕c6

If Black prevents White's next move by 23...a6, then 24.♘e4 is strong. However, it will be seen that once again Black's queen is on a poor square.

24.♘b5   ♘c8

Black is running out of rope. The text is the only way to prevent 25.♘d6, much less 25.♘xa7, which also attacks the queen.

25.♘d4   ...

White's knight continues his tour, now headed for the weakened square f5 – with tempo.

25...   ♕d7

The end is near, no matter what.

26.♘f5   ...

The knight ends his tour with the deadly threat, ♘xh6+.

26...   **h5**

26...♔h7, walking into a discovered check (should White want one) is never very appealing (well, hardly ever!).

27.f4 ...

A strong move which threatens mate. Black has no good defense.

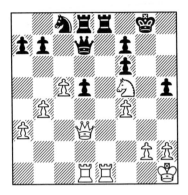

Position after 27.f4

27... 🖻e6?

Black allows the mate, but other moves were not much better:

A) 27...♔h7 (hoping to get in ...🖻e8-g8) 28.♘d6+ winning the exchange.

B) 27...🖻xe1+ (to prevent the above line) 28.🖻xe1 and:

B1) 28...♔h7 when 29.🖻e3 (among others) is strong.
B2) 28...♔f8 29.♘e3 and White is winning, e.g., 29...🖻e8 30.♕h7 🖻e4 31.♕h8+ ♔e7 32.♕xh5.

[C] 27...♔f8 28.h3 🖻e6 29.g4 (White's idea is to support the knight and get a mating attack) 29...hxg4 30.hxg4 ♕e8 31.♕g3 🖻e2 32.🖻xe2 ♕xe2 33.🖻e1 ♕d2 34.♕h4 ♔g8□:

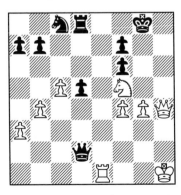

Position after 34...♔g8 (analysis)

And now White gets a winning attack with either:

C1) 35.g5 (prosaic), or
C2) 35.♕xf6 (spectacular)

Analysis with the aid of Mark Lefler's *NOW*.]

After 27...♖e6? White announced mate in three.

28.♕g3+	**♔f8**
29.♕g7+	**♔e8**
30.♕g8#	

A very satisfying victory!

Game 13

"The Old Attacking Game"

The 1969 Merrimac Tournament was a good one for me. I won the "A" prize, $75 and gained an expert's rating with a victory in the penultimate round over future IM Jack Peters [see Game 19]. My best game of the lot was this tactical melee against the Connecticut State Champion, Larry Noderer. After a slow start, a small slip by my opponent allows me to open the floodgates. I consider the attack in this game to be one of my best. It would have been better, however, had I not missed a brilliant line in time trouble [and a strange double blunder on move 29], but since I was already winning this was a harmless omission. Now, on with the game.

Larry Noderer (2100) – Dan Heisman (1926)
Merrimac Grand Prix, New Hampshire 1969
Sicilian Defense

1.e4	c5
2.♘f3	d6
3.d4	cxd4
4.♘xd4	♘f6
5.♘c3	a6
6.h3	...

Black is playing the Najdorf Variation – good enough for Fischer, good enough for me. I expect to garner "a lot" of full points in my chess career with the Najdorf. White plays a rare line and apparently I was more familiar with it than he was.

6...	g6
7.♗g5	...

White's plan is inconsistent. Normal is 7.g4 ♗g7 8.g5 ♘h5! 9.♗e2 e5 followed by ...♘h5-f4 with a good game for Black.

7...	♗g7
8.♕d2	...

White apparently opts for a Dragon, with an extra h2-h3. But I had other ideas.

8...	**♘bd7**
9.g4	**...**

Still mixing ideas.

9...	**b5**
10.♗g2	**♗b7**
11.a3	**...**

Always glad to see a2-a3!

11...	**♕c7**
12.0-0	**...**

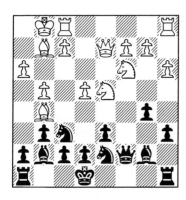

Position after 12.0-0

12...h5

The reason for my delay in castling – I want to put the question to my opponent's weakened kingside pawns.

13.♗xf6	**...**

White decides to close things up – at the cost of his bishop pair.

13...	**♘xf6**
14.g5	**♘d7**
15.♔h1	**...**

White's next few moves revolve around the plan to get in f4 – which would be unfeasible here because of 15...♕c5, winning the piece after 16. "guards the knight," 16...e5. [*R:* 15.♔h1? – better is 15.a4 or 15.♘d5 when Black's advantage is minimal.]

15...	**♘b6**

Black prepares ...♘b6-c4, forcing the queen to c1, where it hinders the development of the rook on a1.

16.♖ad1   **♛c5**

Again, the threat is 17...♘c4 and ...♘xb2.

17.♘b3   **♛c7**
18.♘a5   **...**

White, being higher rated, does not wish to repeat moves.

18...   **♘c4**
19.♘xc4   **♛xc4**
20.♖fe1   **♖ac8**
21.♖e3   **0-0**
22.f4   **...**

About this point I (Black) offered a draw [*R: Are you crazy?!*], and, luckily for me, my opponent did not accept. With the text move, White has achieved his goal. Whether or not the goal was worthwhile is open to question, as can be seen by the game continuation.

22...   **a5**

Black continues logically, with the well known "minority attack." Admittedly, I did not see my opponent's next move, nor the one that followed, creating a dynamic imbalance in the position.

23.♖1e1!   **...**

Active play. If now 23...b4, then 24.♘d5 (or 24.axb4 followed by 25.♘d5), and if 24...♗xd5 25.exd5 ♛xc2 26.♛xc2 ♖xc2 and White has counterchances ⩱. [23.e5 is best according to *Rybka,*, but Black is still much better.]

23...   **♖fe8**

Reactivating the threat of ...b5-b4. [*R: 23...b4!*.]

24.♗f1?!   **...**

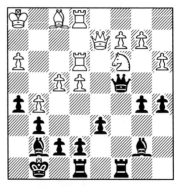

Position after 24.♗f1?!

Admittedly, I did not see this move coming, and at first I thought I had blundered a pawn. However, White forces Black to play a continuation that cannot be bad for Black, as judged by the game. It is hard to suggest an active plan against 24...b4 other than the text.

24...   **♗xc3**

Obviously forced. Because of the closed position on the kingside, Black can give up his fianchettoed bishop.

[*R:* Wrong! 24...♗xc3 is actually not good. After 24...♕c5! White cannot safely take the pawn, e.g. 25.♗xb5? ♗xc3! or 25.♘xb5 ♕xc2 with a big advantage to Black.]

25.bxc3?   **...**

This eventually leads to a lost game. 25.♕xc3? is worse, leading to a lost endgame. My opponent may have rejected 25.♖xc3 because of 25...♗xe4+, but the situation is not entirely clear:

25.♖xc3 ♗xe4+ 26.♔h2 and now:

A) 26...♕e6 27.♗xb5.

B) 26...♕d5 27.♕xd5 ♗xd5 28.♖xc8 ♖xc8, and after 29.c3 White threatens 30.♗xb5. Or

C) 26...♕a4? 27.b3 and White wins a piece.

Also interesting after 25.♖xc3 is an immediate 25...♕a4, e.g., 26.b3 ♕xa3 27.♗xb5 with an unclear position.

25...   **♕c5**
26.♖b1   **...**

White wants to work on the "backward" b-pawn. His plan does not work because he does not realize that his king is in danger. If White plays passively, Black can work on the weak queenside pawns with good prospects of winning.

26...   **♗c6**

Now White has trouble putting more pressure on the b-pawn, as ♕d2-d3 does not threaten anything. The black bishop now has two excellent diagonals at its disposal: The long one (a8-h1) and h3-c8 after ...♗d7 (moving the bishop to double rooks on the c-file).

27.♖b3?   **...**

White does not sense the danger so he protects the a-pawn, hoping to double at some later time along the b-file.

27...   **♕f5!**

This move wins. The white pawns are now shown to be weak in their advanced positions. There is no defense to both ...♕xf4 and ...♗xe4+, so White decides to keep material even, but the exposed position of White's king should soon prove fatal.

[*R:* 27...e5! is also winning.]

28.♖xb5 **...**

Taking advantage of the black bishop's defense of the queen.

28... **♕xf4**

Now, because the rook is attacked, White must allow ...♗xe4+, and White is sure to lose.

29.♖xa5?? **♗xe4+??**

A case of double chess blindness. Both players are so caught up in clever pins and overworked pieces that they overlook a piece *en prise*. Everyone to whom I showed this game has overlooked 29...♕xf1+! – this includes Coach IM Donald Byrne and NM Richard Pariseau, among others! The hanging bishop was finally noticed while showing this game at Penn State to Jim Joachim and Frank Gavlak, one year after it was played!!

30.♗g2 **...**

What else? On 30.♔g1 Black can play ...♗xc2 or the quiet ...♖b8. [*R:* 30...d5 is best, and winning.] However, 30.♔b1 would be better than the text, although White can hardly be blamed for missing Black's next move.

30... **♖xc3!!**

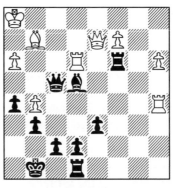

Position after 30...♖xc3!!

Now White is helpless:

A) 31.♗xe4 ♖xe3 with the threat of ...♖xh3+ winning the queen.

B) 31.♖xe4 ♕xd2.

C) 31.♖xc3 ♕xd2.

D) 31.♕xc3 ♕f1+! 32. ♔h2 ♕xg2#.

31.♖e2?   **...**

White falters under the pressure. He must protect the queen, but he must also protect the third rank, so better would be 31.♖d3. Then Black can play 31...♕xd2 32.♖xd2 ♖xh3+ 33.♔g1 ♗xg2 34.♔xg2 ♖c3 with an easy win. The game continuation, on the other hand, gives Black a chance for a nice finish.

31...	**♖xh3+**
32.♔g1	**♕h2+**
33.♔f1	**♗xg2+(?)**

The move played wins easily enough, but Black could have finished beautifully with 33...♖b8!!:

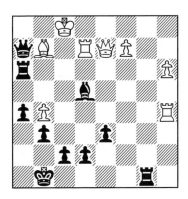

Position after 33...♖b8!! (analysis)

A) 34.♗xh3 ♖b1+ 35.♖e1 ♕xd2.

B) 34.♗xe4 ♖b1+ 35.♖e1 ♕xd2.

C) 34.♖xe4 ♖f3+! 35.♔e1 (35.♗xf3 ♕xd2) 35...♕g1+, etc.

[R: Both moves are winning, but 33...♗xg2+ is "better."]

34.♖xg2	**♖f3+**
35.♖f2	**♖b8**

Not as powerful now as on the 33rd move, but still more than sufficient.

36.♕d4 ...

Nothing else. If 36.♕e1 ♖b1.

36... ♕g3?

36...♖xf2+ 37.♕xf2 ♕h1+ 38.♔e2 ♕e4+ is more forcing, as the rook soon enters the attack.

37.♔e2 ...

Fortunately, White still has no play.

37... ♖xf2+
38.♕xf2 ♕c3

Now the win is clear. Although Black has been in time trouble for some moves now, the win was always easy. I wish all such time troubles were so easy! At this point I said "That's a hard move to meet!" and Mr. Noderer replied, "All your moves are hard to meet." A fine compliment and a sporting gesture on Mr. Noderer's part. The rest needs no comment!

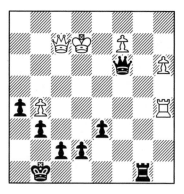

Position after 38...♕c3

39.♖a7	♕xc2+
40.♔f1	♕c1+
41.♕e1	♕f4+
42.♔e2	♕e4+
43.♔f2	♖b2+
0-1	

Mate in a few.

Game 14

Kingside Attack!

This analysis, as well as that for Game 16, was originally written as an assignment for a Penn State Philosophy 430 class – a class in Chess Analysis taught by International Master (and normally English professor) Donald Byrne. For the enlightenment of the reader, I will give Byrne's comments to my notes in braces, "{" and "}", with Professor Byrne's permission. Also, as I improved I realized how important time usage was, so I started to record my time; elapsed time in this 50 moves in 2-hour game for Black are shown after Black's moves in parentheses.

After a long layoff – one tournament in nine months – I returned home expecting to be in poor form. However, I defeated Rich Pariseau and Don Latzel in two of the best games I have played to date. Both of these games occurred shortly after the start of summer vacation. True, I was shortly to slump to my usual "early summer" form, but at least I proved to myself that I can play well at certain times of the year, hitherto thought to be my "off-form" periods.

Don Latzel (1950) – Dan Heisman (1920)
Germantown Chess Club Ladder Game
Philadelphia 1970
Nimzo-Indian Defense
(50 moves in 2 hours)

1.d4 ...

Latzel has beaten me more times in slow games than any other player. This was the first time, however, that he had played 1.d4 against me.

1...	**♘f6**
2.c4	**e6**
3.♘c3	**♗b4**

And this was the first time that I had played this defense against anyone – and with what results! I only regret that this makes it hard to pull off a decent encore.

4.e3 ...

The most popular, Rubinstein Variation.

4... **b6**

A move that was brought to my attention by the young British theoreticians.

5.♘e2 ...

Most usual is 5.♗d3, but 5.♘e2 is becoming an increasingly popular alternative.

5...   **♗a6**
6.a3   **♗e7**
7.b3   ...

The first deviation from standard play. 7.♘f4 is the normal move and German theoretician Schwarz gives 7.♘g3 a "(?)." {Byrne's comment: Why is 7.♘g3 a bad move?}

The idea of 7.b3 is usually an eventual ♗c1-b2. For instance, *MCO-10* gives 7.b3 d5 8.♗b2 O-O 9.♘f4 followed by 9...c6 10.♗d3 given in the game Botvinnik-Novotyelnov, USSR Championship 1951. However, the note says, "better is 9...dxc4 10.bxc4 ♘bd7," which is interesting since I, with no knowledge of these notes, followed the suggestion. There is a big difference, however: Latzel is apparently not planning an early ♗c1-b2 – either that or else he felt that he really never had time for this move.

7...   **d5**
8.♘f4   **O-O** (10)

Ten minutes total time used by Black. And so we reach a position which can transpose into the *MCO* suggestion after 9.♗b2. Latzel feels that it is more important to castle first and this is possibly too slow.

9.♗d3   **dxc4**

I waited for the bishop to move before capturing the pawn so that White would not have the option of developing the bishop with tempo.

10.bxc4   **♘bd7** (15)

Here it can be seen that I am following the "better" idea of ...dxc4 followed by ...♘bd7.

11.O-O   ...

Apparently, this was White's best chance to play ♗c1-b2, although the answer would be the same. {Explain the advantage of ♗b2.}

11...   **e5** (17)

Thematic. The game is starting to take shape. Black is about to strike at White's center in order to force White to declare his intentions. Notice that Black is already better developed.

12 .♘4d5   **...**

I did not expect this answer! I had only considered 12.♘4e2. It seems that 12.♘h5 is not very strong; however, placing the knight on d5 allows a further sharp thrust for Black in the center. It is useless to analyze all the possible lines after 12.♘h5 or 12.♘4e2 because they are not important to the general theme of this game. {But you should give a likely line in each case.}

12...   **c5! (22)**

I gladly part with the two bishops. White's next few replies are either best or forced. The only aspect of these lines that made me reluctant to proceed this way was that White will get a strong protected passed pawn, never something I gladly allow.

13.♘xe7+   **♛xe7**
14.d5   **...**

The only move. Obviously, on 14.dxe5 or 14.dxc5, Black will recapture with the knight, followed by the appropriate rook to d8, with an attack on the very weak white c-pawn. Also, Black was threatening to take the d-pawn with either pawn.

14...   **e4 (24)**

This pawn will prove a thorn in White's side. Ironically enough, both Latzel and I rejected (over the board) his chance to capture this pawn later, which by post-game analysis seemed to be his last chance of saving the game.

15.♗e2   **♘e5 (25)**
16.♛b3   **...**

Apparently better than 16.♛a4, after which Black's best try seems to be 16...♗c8, for then Black's problems on the queenside are not nearly as great as in the game. White instead logically strives for his queenside break, a4-a5.

16...   **♖ad8 (38)**

The first important move of the game – notice my time for the move. The reason I took so long (at 50 moves in 2 hours, 13 minutes is pretty long for me) is not that I was considering the alternative ...♗a6-c8, but that I was trying to evolve my game plan. My original idea stared me in the face: get the knight on f6 to d6 in order to first blockade the passed pawn and secondly put great pressure on White's c-pawn. However, there is no tactical justification to such a maneuver: 16...♘e8? 17.♘xe4 and now 17...♘xc4 loses a piece to 18.♗xc4 ♛xe4 19.♗xa6.

So, the problem becomes: What else can I do? Certainly 16...♖ad8 detracts from my queenside defense. The black queen's rook later participates in some lines of play that occur only in the notes. However, the same job can be done by 16...♖fd8, which is therefore better than the text. The reason is that after White plays a4-a5, I can play my rook on a8 to c8 after playing ...bxa5. Then after ♖xa5 for White, I will have my bishop removed as in the game and White's queenside attack is less potent. Another possibility is that I will try to hold my a- or b-pawns with my queen and rook. Yet another possible move is 16...♗c8, resulting in lines similar to the game, but with "a little less attack on both sides." Maybe 16...♗c8 is good, but it would probably have been a lot less exciting.

17.a4 ...

As was indicated, the logical follow-up to 16.♕b3. Of course, 17.♗b2 is playable, but then White's counterattack is much slower. Also, after 17.a4, White has the choice whether to develop the bishop on either b2 or a3, though at the moment b2 certainly seems superior.

17... ♗c8 (46)

A valuable eight minutes. In this nothing-to-lose club game, I now smell white king blood and I'm determined to pull off a kingside attack. And, as Kavalek would say, "with a little help from my friends" [a reference to a *Chess Life* article GM Lubomir Kavalek wrote around this time] – it works great.

18.a5 ...

Having said "a," or rather a4, White now says "b," a5. Certainly after 17.a4, 18.a5 is best.

18... ♘6g4?! (54)

Here I come! But the "?" before the "!" indicates something is clearly wrong – and that is true. Despite the eight minutes spent on this move, I couldn't begin to see that my pawn sacrifice was unsound. By this I don't mean that my analysis of White's reply 19.axb6 was incorrect, as will be seen from the game continuation, but rather that indeed, White could play 19.♘xe4!! (one exclamation point for strength, another for "guts"). Apparently, with 19.♘xe4!! White actually equalizes or gets the better game. I had not overlooked this move (of course), but during the game I spent my eight minutes reasoning thusly:

"What if he takes axb6? Then I surely lose a pawn, so I'd better be careful when analyzing this move. On the other hand, if he takes 19.♘xe4 he seems to be losing time on the queenside (where his attack is). Also, I seem to have two very strong replies: 19...♕h4 and 19...♘xh2. They both seem strong, so one of them is almost undoubtedly sound. So if 19.axb6 fails for White, then I'll play 18...♘6g4." I therefore proceeded to take most of my time analyzing 19.axb6, which I found to be inadequate for White. And so I played 18...♘6g4. {If Black does not play this move, what are the alternatives?} There came the sharp reply:

19.axb6(?)   ...

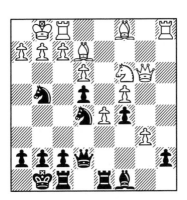

Position after 19.axb6(?)

Accepting the challenge. But it was certainly difficult to see that 19.♘xe4!! was the last chance to save White's game:

A) 19...♕h4 20.h3:

A1) 20...♘xf2?? (hoping to snare the hanging ♘ on e4) 21.♘xf2.

A2) 20...♘xe3?? 21.♕xe3.

A3) 20...♘f6 21.♘xf6+ gxf6 22.♔h2 is safe.

A4) 20...♘h6 21.f4

A4a) 21...♘g6 22.♘f2.
A4b) 21...♘5g4 22.hxg4 ♗xg4 23.♕d1 ♗xe2 24.♕xe2 ♘g4 25.g3 △ ♕g2.
A4c) 21...♗xh3 22.fxe5 ♗xg2 (22...♕xe4 23.hxg3) 23.♔xg2 ♕xe4+ 24.♗f3 (or 24.♔f2).
... and in none of these lines does Black have better than a forced draw at any point.

A5) 20...♘h2 21.♔xh2 ♕xe4 and now White could even play 22.axb6 with probable immunity. If not, 22.f3 is safe. Either way, White is up in material.

B) 19...♘xh2 20.♔xh2 ♕h4+ 21.♔g1:

B1) 21...♕xe4 22.axb6 is probably safe:

B1a) 22...♗h3?! 23.gxh3 ♖d6 (23...♘f3+ 24.♗xf3 ♕xf3 25.♔h2! ♖d6 26.♖g1 ♖h6 27.♖g3+−) 24.f4 ♖g6+ 25.♔f2 ♖g2+ 26.♔e1.
B1b) 22...axb6 23.♕xb6 f5 is too slow.

B2) 21...♗g4?!? (an offhand suggestion by Steve Wexler, Penn State's 2nd board) 22.f3

B2a) 22...♗h3 23.g3 with the idea of 24.♖f2.
B2b) 22...f5 23.fxg4

B2bi) 23...fxg4 24.g3 ♕h3 25.♗b2.
B2bii) 23...♘xg4 24.♗xg4 fxg4 25.♘f2. In this last line, an amusing sample line might be 25...♖xf2!? 26.♖xf2 g3 27.♖f4 ♕h2+ 28.♔f1 ♕h1+ 29.♔e2 ♕xg2+ 30.♔d3 ♕h3 (if 30...♕h2 31. ♖a2 g2 32. ♖4f2 +−) 31.♗b2 (at last!) 31...g2 32.♕c3 ♕g3 33.♖g1 ♖e8(?) 34.♕xg7+, so I can't resist adding that one cannot blame Latzel for missing 34.♕xg7+ when deciding against 19.♘xe4!!. Oh, well, back to the ranch (club).

[Sometimes it is not so easy to prove which was the losing move!]

19...   ♘f3+! (60)

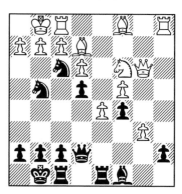

Position after 19...♘f3+!

Only! This apparently came as a surprise to White. No use analyzing other moves for Black.

20.♗xf3   ...

Forced. Both 20.gxf3 and 20.♔h1 meet with rapid disaster:

A) 20.gxf3? exf3:

A1) 21.Bishop any but ♗xf3: 21...♕h4 and mate.

A2) 21.♗xf3 ♕h4 22.h3(!) (to give White the h2 escape square;

if immediately 22.♗xg4 ♕xg4+ 23.♔h1 ♕f3+ 24.♔g1 ♗h3 and mates) 22...♕xh3 23.♗xg4 ♕xg4+ and now:

A2a) 24.♔h2 ♖d6 25.e4 ♖g6 26.♗g5 (shades of the W. Weinstein vs. Fischer controversy) [a reference to a Soviet Master who found fault with a Fischer analysis by finding a saving interpolative move] 26...♕h3+ 27.♔g1 ♖xg5#.

A2b) 24.♔h1 ♕f3+ with lines the same as in i.

B) 20.♔h1 ♕h4 21.h3 ♘xf2+ 22.♖xf2 ♕xf2 23.gxf3 (or 23.♗b2 ♗xh3 and wins, or 23.♕d1 ♗xh3 24.♕f1 ♗xg2+! 25.♕xg2 ♕h4+ and mates) 23...♗xf3 and wins (23...exf3 also wins).

20...	exf3
21.h3	...

A hard decision. White foresees that h2-h3 will undoubtedly be necessary in the near future so he decides to play it now, hoping the knight will retreat. White has four tries other than 21.h3: A) 21.g3, B) 21.♘e4, C) 21.gxf3, and D) 21.bxa7!.

A) Definitely worse than 21.h3 is 21.g3 ♘xh2! and now:

A1) 22.♔xh2? ♕d7!. A unique maneuver with mate forthcoming, e.g., 23.♖h1 ♕h3+ 24.♔g1 ♕g2#.

A2) 22.bxa7? ♕d7 23.a8♕ ♕h3.

A3) 22.♖e1! ♕d7 23.♘e2! and now *not*

A3a) 23...fxe2 24.♔xh2 ♕h3+ 25.♔g1 ♗g4 26.e4, nor
A3b) 23...♕h3 24.♘f4, *but...*
A3c) 23...g5!! with the threat of 24...♕h3 and White has run out of defenses:

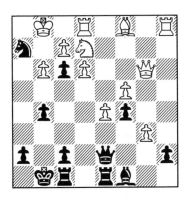

Position after 23...g5!! (analysis)

A last try for White (in the line 21.g3 ♘xh2) is:

A4) 22.♕b5!? (to stop 22...♕d7). Black seems to have many reasonable variations, e.g.,

A4a) 22...♘xf1

A4ai) 23.bxa7 ♗h3.

A4aii) 23.♔xf1 ♕f6!? 24.bxa7 (24.♗b2 ♕xb6) 24...♕xc3 25. ♗b2 (25. a8♕? ♕d3+ 26.♔g1 ♕d1+ 27.♔h2 ♕f1 and mates) 25...♕d3+ 26.♔g1 ♕f5! 27.♔f1 (27.a8♕?? ♕h3 mates) 27...♖d6!! (27...♗d7 is also possible) 28.♕b3! (28.a8♕? ♖h3 29.♔e1 ♕d3) 28...♖h6 (again 28...♗d7 is possible) 29.♔e1 ♖h1+ 30.♔d2 ♖xa1 31.♗xa1 ♗a6 32.♕b8 ♕c8 33.a8♕ at last! (not 33.♕e5 f6) 33...♕xb8 34.♕xa6 ♕b1 35.d6?! ♕f1 36.d7 ♕xf2+ 37. ♔d1 ♕e2+ 38.♔c1 ♕xe3+ 39.♔c2 f2 40.♕c8 f1♕ (also winning is 40...♕e7 △ 41...f1♕ −+), and:

- 41.♕xf8+ ♔xf8 42.d8♕+ (his third different queen!!!) 42...♕e8 43.♗xg7+ ♔xg7 44.♕xe8 (not 44.♕g5+?? ♔h8) 44...♕xc4+ −+ .
- 41.d8♕ ♕1c1 mate!

A4b) 22...♕f6. A variation worth looking into, but perhaps you've seen enough lines in this variation!

Finally, other White 21st moves (instead of the game's 21.h3) are:

B) 21.♘e4 ♕h4 22.h3 transposing into the game.

C) 21.gxf3? ♕h4 22.fxg4 (22.♖d1? ♕xh2+ 23.♔f1 ♕f2#) 22...♕xg4+ 23.♔h1 ♕f3+ 24.♔h1 ♗h3 and mate.

D) Giving the most trouble may be 21.bxa7! ♕h4 22.h3 fxg2 23.♔xg2 (not 23.a8♕ ♕xh3 and mate) when Black has only one clearly good reply:

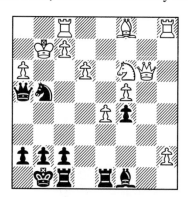

Position after 23.♔xg2 (analysis)

D1) 23...♘e5? 24.♖h1 +–.

D2) 23...♘xf2 24.♖xf2 (24.a8♕? ♗xh3+ –+) 24...♗xh3+ 25. ♔g1 ♕g3+ 26.♔h1 ♕xf2 27.♖a2! and White, with eventual threats of ♘b5 and ♘c7, has slight chances, e.g., 27...♕e1+ 28.♔h2 ♕xc1 29.♘b5, although, of course, Black should win with some care.

Clear and forcing, though, is:

D3) 23...♘xe3+! and

D3a) 24.♔f3 ♕xh3+ is easy enough. If 25.♔e4 to avoid losing the king's rook with check, 25...♖fe8+ is deadly.
D3b) 24.fxe3 ♗xh3+ 25.♔f3 (25.♔g1?? ♕g3+ and ♕g2#) 25...♗xf1 with continued threats.
D3c) 24.♗xe3 ♗xh3+ 25.♔h1 (or 25.♔h2, but not 25.♔g1 ♕g4+ and ♕g2# or 25.♔f3 ♕g4#) 25...♗xf1+ 26.♔g1 ♗xc4 (or 26...♗h3).

21...   **♕h4** (76)

Only 16 minutes for this move! Black threatens 22...fxg2, which is a hard move to stop. Of course, 22.gxf3 ♕xh3 has been shown in earlier notes (move 20, line A2) to be hopeless. But now there are fewer tries at defense: 22.bxa7, then he transposes into notes given above after 22...fxg2, e.g., 23.♔xg2 ♘xe3+ (note D3), etc. But the way White plays it makes the win elementary. Then again, one must admit he has been in great danger for the past few moves – ever since he missed 19.♘xe4!!, which can now be appreciated for both its exclamation points.

22.♘e4   **...**

Nothing saves the day. It looks logical to bring the knight to the defense, but it "hangs" on e4, and thus allows a simple combination.

22...   **fxg2** (78)

That took only two minutes. White's reply is forced.

23.♔xg2   **♘e5** (81)

Now the defense 24.♖h1 (not the same as move 21, note D1, because Black has used a tempo to play ♘e5) fails to 24...♕xe4+.

24.f4   **...**

The only other defense, 24.f3, fails to 24...♗xh3+ 25.♔g1 ♖d6!:

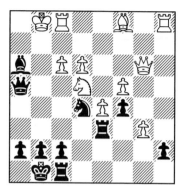

Position after 25...罝d6! (analysis)

The rook finally shows some gusto with the unstoppable threat of 25...罝g3+. Of course, 26.公xd6 is the needed deflection to allow 26...豐g3+ and 27...豐g2#. Finally, if 26.罝f2 罝g6+ 27.曮h1 盫g2+ 28.曮g1 豐h1#.

24...   **盫xh3+**

The waters clear. White is (has been) dead.

25.曮g1   **豐g4+**

The queen now penetrates. 26.曮f2 豐g2+ picks up the rook next move with check yet, so...

0-1

Moral of the game: Ken Boehm, with his pawn-snatching style, would never overlook 19.公xe4!! unless he thought that 19.axb6 would win two pawns!

{Byrne's final comment: Once the attack is under way, your analysis is sharp, but before that you do not do much to illuminate the game. Consider this question, for I think that it points to a basic problem. If you played this line again, would you change your procedure at any point?}

Game 15

Expert Technique

Some of the games I play I don't appreciate until many years later. Certainly, this is the case of my game when I was a 1385 rated player against local high school "B" player Tim Strauch, where I played as well after the opening as I ever do. I just didn't realize how well I could play, since I had no experience to compare my play to an expert or a master. In this game from a Wilmington C.C. vs. Germantown C.C. match, I beat the promising Bruce Baker. As one would expect in a game between a 2000 player and an 1800 player [Bruce shortly thereafter became a highly respected master himself], it is hardly flawless. Yet the 2000 player's superior defense and positional judgement happen to show through in this game very nicely. My only missed sequence came in time trouble when my opponent was lost anyway. So let's see how I accumulate little positional advantages by avoiding tactical tricks.

B. Baker (~1850) – D. Heisman (2060)
Wilmington C.C. vs. Germantown C.C. Match
Wilmington, Delaware 1970
Sicilian Defense

1.e4	c5
2.♘f3	d6
3.d4	cxd4
4.♘xd4	♘f6
5.♘c3	a6

Much as I distrust the Najdorf, I feel pretty comfortable on both sides and I get good results. Add to this the fact that I am more "booked" in this than any other opening, and one can conclude that 5...a6 should be good for me.

6.♗e2   ...

By now, I was becoming accustomed to the "quiet" 6.♗e2 and this was probably the first game I had played wherein I knew the book better than my opponent.

6...   **e5**

Of course, 6...e6 is playable, but hardly in the *spirit* of the Najdorf. (See game 7.)

7.♘f3   **...**

This is not considered to be as good as 7.♘b3 because it blocks White's kingside expansion with f4-f5.

7...   **♗e7**

This is *MCO's* move. GM O'Kelly says 7...♕c7 or 7...h6 are good answers to 7.♘f3.

8.0-0   **0-0**
9.♗g5   **...**

Still following the *MCO* line.

9...   **♗e6**

MCO-10 says 9...♘bd7 10. a4 h6 11.♗e3 ♕c7 12.♘d2 b6 13.♗c4 ♗b7 14.♕e2 ♘c5 15.f3 ♖fd8 16.♘d5 ♘xd5= Bannik-Krogius, USSR. Championship 1963. Possibly the reason that 9...♘bd7 is better than 9...♗e6 is the sequence 10.♗xf6 ♗xf6 11.♘d5 ♗xd5 12.♕xd5, when White captures on the d5 square without putting a pawn on it.

10.♕d2   **...**

Typically aiming for pressure on the d-pawn which, of course, should never materialize.

10...   **b5**

Typically expanding on the queenside. Of course, 10...♘bd7 can be considered first [...and *Rybka* greatly prefers that].

11.a3   **...**

Usually a waste of time in the Najdorf, this move can be condoned here because of the threat 11...b4 12.♘d5 ♗xd5 13.exd5 ♘d7 and Black stands better. If 11.♖ad1, Black can simply play 11...♘bd7.

11...   **♘bd7**
12.♖ad1   **♕c7**

Black is making more or less automatic moves while White will begin searching for a plan, and he will soon cede the initiative to Black. White normally tries for f4-f5, but since this is not feasible, he tries for pressure on the center. Black, meanwhile, is almost ready for certain queenside action. [*Rybka* thinks 12...h6 first is much more accurate here and on the next move.]

13.♖fe1   **♖fd8**

The right rook to the right square. Black prepares to free his bishop from having to protect the d-pawn by moving the knight to either to c5 or b6, the latter with either an eye to ...d6-d5 or ...♘c4.

14.h3 ...

White is running low on moves so he waits.

14... **♘b6**

Plan "B" goes into effect. Black's game is threatening to turn excellent, so White decides to act.

15.♗xf6 **♗xf6**
16.♘d5 ...

This sequence is almost always advantageous for Black if White must put a pawn on d5.

Position after 16.♘d5

16... **♗xd5**

The correct way. On 16...♘xd5 17.exd5 Black's bishop pair is worthless. Here the knight puts pressure on the d-pawn with an eye on c4. Despite opposite-colored bishops, Black now has the advantage. Now the tactical threats start, which last for the rest of the game.

17.exd5 **♖ac8**

This is more accurate than 17...♘c4, which takes the knight immediately off the d-pawn. [*Rybka* prefers 17...e4 or 17...♖e8.]

18.c3 ...

Creates the necessary weaknesses on the queenside for Black to exploit. But of course 18.♗d3 g6! is very strong for Black. Not 18...♘xd5?

19.♗f5 +– (but not 19.♗xh7+? ♔xh7 20.♕xd5 ♕xc2 and Black stands better).

18...   **♕b7**

Good! Black prepares to pursue a minority attack (...a6-a5, ...b5-b4) while piling pressure on the d-pawn. White's following moves, attempting to relocate his pieces while protecting the d-pawn, are nicely refuted.

19.♘h2   **...**

White pants to put the knight on g4 and the bishop on f3. He rightly feels his chances lie on the kingside.

19...   **♖c5**

A strong move, increasing pressure simultaneously on the bishop file and the d-pawn.

20.♘g4?!   **...**

Consistent and cute, but dubious. After the more prosaic 20. ♗f3 the game might continue 20...g6! 21.♘g4 ♗g7, and the threat of ...f7-f5 gives Black a distinct advantage.

20...   **♗e7**

The text avoids the complications of 20...♖xd5 21.♘xf6+ gxf6. Of course, 20...♘xd5 21.♘xf6+ gxf6 22.♗f3 is painful for Black.

21.♘e3   **...**

Now the drawback of 20.♘g4 is obvious. If 21.♗f3, then 21...f5 is very embarrassing to White. The test is refuted very nicely. [*Rybka* prefers 21.♗d3 g6 with a small but clear advantage to Black.]

Position after 21.♘e3

21... &g5!!

The best move of the game. By moving the bishop again, Black practically paralyzes White.

22.♕c2 ...

Getting out of the pin and hoping for 22...&xe3 23.fxe3 ♘xd5 24.&f3.

22... g6!

Another shot. Since Black has the only dark-squared bishop, this idea of ...f7-f5 is very strong. Also, the bishop can now retreat to g7 if necessary.

23.&f3 ...

Finally! But now one can see that White's plan has proven fruitless. Black has the advantage on all three sectors of the board. [*Rybka* prefers 23.g4 when Black retains a nice advantage.]

23... a5

Black has plenty of play. He now initiates a minority attack, with the moves ...f7-f5 and ...♖8c8 in hand. [*R:* 23...f5 immediately is better.]

24.♕d3 ...

Probably inaccurate, but White is understandably anxious. Another idea is 24.♖d2, for if 24...&xe3? 25.fxe3 ♘xd5 26.♕d3!.

24... ♘a4

Attacking b2 and c3 and preparing an upcoming ...b5-b4. [Again 24...f5!.]

25.♖e2?? ...

The losing error. Necessary was 25.♖d2, whereupon Black has his choice of an immediate ...b5-b4 or a slower plan with ...♖8c8 and ...f7-f5.
[*R:* One question mark is plenty. Better is 25.♕c2, but 25.♖e2 only deteriorates the White position a little more.]

25... f5

Rather aesthetic. White's four pieces are no match for the black f- and e-pawns. Black now wins a piece, so White tries to give it up in the best way possible.

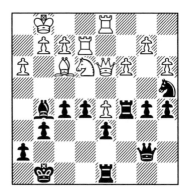

Position after 25...f5

26.♘xf5   ...

26.h4 could come under consideration. If then 26...♗xh4?! 27.g3 e4 (if the bishop moves, ♗f3-g2 saves the piece) 28.♗xe4 fxe4 29.♕xe4 ♗g5 (29...♗f6 30.♘g4) when Black manages to hold a winning position.

26...   **gxf5**
27.♕xf5   **♕e7**

Although this walks into a pin on the e-file, 27...♕g7 is bad because of the alignment on the g-file after 28.♖e4.

28.h4   ...

[The silicon brain judges 28.♕c2 to be preferable, but Black is well ahead.]

28...   **♗h6**

Black is in no hurry to create complications. After 28...♗xh4 29.♖d4 he still must defend carefully. [*R:* Not correct. 28...♗xh4! is best, and if 29.♖d4 then 29...♔h8 and Black is winning.]

29.♖d4   **♖c4**

Forcing the trade of the inactive rook for an active one. [*Rybka* points out that 29...♖c4? loses a key pawn to 30.♖xc4 bxc4 31.♕g4+.]

30.♖2e4   ...

[? – Missing that simple win of a pawn.]

30....   **♘xb2**

Defending the rook and winning a pawn.

31.♖xc4   ...

Perhaps it was better for White first to play 31.♖g4+.

31...   **♘xc4**
32.♖g4+   **♔h8**

And not 32...♗g7 33.h5, when Black must play 33...♔h8 anyway, since on 33...h6? 34.♗e4 is strong as Black's light squares would be weak.

33.♕h5   ...

[33.a4 is best, but it can't save the game now.]

33...   **♕f6**

33...♗d2!? is an interesting alternative.

34.♗e4   ...

White threatens 35.♗g6!, winning.

34...   **♖g8(!)**

A finely calculated move. [*R:* It may be finely calculated but it's an error. Much better is 34...♖f8 with an easy win.]

35.♖xg8+   **♔xg8**
36.♕e8+   ...

The same type of problems confronts both sides after 36.♕g4+.

36...   **♕f8**

If 36...♔g7 37.♕d7+ and Black loses the h-pawn or takes his queen off the protection of the d-pawn. [36...♗f8 is best, according to *Rybka*.]

37.♕e6+   ...

[Somewhat better are 37.♕d7 or 37.♕xb5 ♖d2 38.♗c2.]

37...   **♔h8**
38.♕d7   ...

With his last two moves White wins a tempo with a mate threat.

38...   **♗g7**
39.h5   ...

With an obvious threat.

39...   **♕g8**

A safe bunch in the corner. [*R:* Throwing away much of Black's advantage. Preferable were 39...♘d2 or 39...♕f6.]

40.♕xb5   **♘d2**

Not 40...♘xa3?? 41.♕b3 and White may even win.

41.♗c2   **...**

If 41.♗f5, with the idea of ♗e6, then 41...e4 is still good.

41...   **e4(!)**

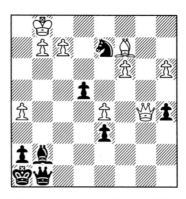

Position after 41...e4(!)

Black increases the scope of his pieces.

42.♕e2?   **...**

A bad mistake which loses any initiative. Better is 42.♕xa5 and there still is a fight as 42...♘f3+ 43.♔f1! is ineffective for Black, so Black must rely on either 42...♗e5, 42...♕c8 or 42...♕f7!?.

[*R:* 42.♕xa5 is the only move. Black can try 42...♕f8, 42...♗e5, or 42...h4, but is not that close to winning.]

42...   **♗xc3**

A strong and simple answer. [*Rybka* notes that 42...♕xd5! is the best refutation of 42.♕e2?.]

43.♗xe4(?)   **...**

"Moves we like to see." [*R:* 43.♕e3! must be tried, when after 43... ♕g7 Black is likely winning but no so easily.]

43...   **♕e8**

Time for White to resign.

44. f3(?)   **...**

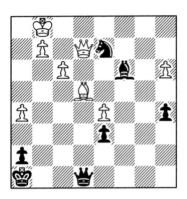

Position after 44.f3

44...	♕e5?!

Stupid! Maybe White wasn't wrong in "missing" resigning. I miss 44...♗d4+ 45.♔h2 ♕xh5+. (Actually, the text may be stronger as there is no good defense to ...♗d4+ and ...♕xh5#.)

45.g4	♕g3+
46.♔h1	♕h3+
47.♕h2	...

47.♔g1 ♗d4+.

47...	♕f1+
48.♕g1	♕h3+
49.♕h2	...

Time trouble. ⊕

49...	♕xh2+
50.♔xh2	♘xe4
51.fxe4	a4(!)
0-1	

Every pawn push in the center is met with a king move: 52.♔g3 ♗b2 53.♔f4 ♗xa3 54.♔e3 (54.e5 ♔g8 or 54...dxe5 with the idea of an eventual ...♗xd6) 54...♗b2 55.♔d3 a3 56.♔c2 ♗e5 57.♔b3 ♔g7 58.g5 ♗f4 59.g6 hxg6 60.hxg6 ♔xg6 61.♔xa3 ♔f6 62.♔b3 ♔e5 63.♔b4 ♔xe4 64.♔c4 ♔e5 *finis.*

Game 16

Straightforward

The following game is no masterpiece. It is not spectacular; in fact, it is rather dull. There are no speculative sacrifices, long combinations, or unclear plans. The blunders are obvious and the technique shown is not difficult. So why did I choose this game to annotate? Because I love it. The game is unique. It is clear and straightforward. The game is beautiful and the beauty lies in its simplicity. I acquired pressure, increased it with the help of a frustrated opponent, broke through, and won easily. If only life were so simple! Reminder: Coach Byrne's comments are given in "{}".

Dan Heisman (1950) – Jerry Kolker (2100)
Practice Game, Pennsylvania 1969
Sicilian Defense

| 1.e4 | c5 |
| 2.♘f3 | ♘c6 |

Jerry Kolker, a very good friend and mentor, *always* plays the Najdorf, if possible. The reason for 2...♘c6 (a signal that it is not a Najdorf) is not really psychological. It will be explained later.

3.d4	cxd4
4.♘xd4	♘f6
5.♘c3	d6
6.♗c4	...

The Sozin, or Fischer, variation. Another fun variation is 6.♗e3 ♘g4 if Black does not wish to transpose into the Dragon.

| 6... | e6 |
| 7.O-O | ... |

A sign of the times. Perhaps today I would play 7.♗e3 with the idea of 8.♕e2 followed by queenside castling: The Velimirović Attack, very popular today among grandmasters. The idea, of course, is to play an early g4-g5 with a quick kingside assault. This idea I carried out successfully in a game against Jim Joachim, one of my friends on our strong Penn State chess team 1969-1971.

7...   ♗d7

Another modern-type move. This thematic idea in the regular Sicilian is to play ...♘xd4 followed by ...♗c6 with pressure on the white d-pawn. This sort of maneuver was successfully(?) carried out against me by ♗ent Larsen during a simultaneous exhibition in Philadelphia (1969), which I managed to draw.

8.♔h1   ...

My king wants no part of the a7-g1 diagonal. I also wish to push the f-pawn. Another way of playing the white pieces is 8.♗e3 or even 8.♗f4 transposing into a variation of the Richter-Rauzer Attack. But those are other games!

8...   ♗e7

Solid and passive. More active moves are 8...♘a5 and 8...♕b6. But understandably, Black does not wish to be *two* moves away from kingside castling while still trying to mix it up in the center.

9.f4   ...

Consistent. Other plans are 9.♗e3 or 9.♗b3, the latter probably best met by 9...♘a5.

9...   ♘xd4

This or 9...O-O, threatening 10...♘xe4, are both okay. The immediate 9...♘xe4 10.♘xe4 d5 seems premature since either 11. ♗xd5 exd5 12.♘c3 with pressure on the d-pawn, or 11.♗d3 dxe4 12.♗xe4 with queenside pressure, or even the speculative 11.♘b5 gives White too much leeway in controlling the game. Therefore, after 9...O-O, White should probably reply 10.♗b3 after which the position is roughly equal.

10.♕xd4   O-O
11.f5   ...

White wants pressure on the e6 square.

11...   e5?

Weak. The hole at d5 and the backward d-pawn allow White to build up pressure. Of course Black based his decision on the fact that he wished to play ...♗c6 and that this was immediately impossible, whereas now ...♗c6 strikes at a fixed target. Also, White may have kingside attacking possibilities if he can permanently prevent Black from playing d5.

12.♕d3 ...

White naturally wishes to keep an eye on both d5 and e4.

12... **♗c6**
13.♘d5 ...

White immediately puts the question to Black and gets a desirable reply. Also possible was 13.♗e3 or better yet 13.♗g5, a thematic move to increase the pressure at d5.

13... **♘xd5**
14.♗xd5 **♗xd5**
15.♕xd5 ...

Weak squares are, of course, meant to be occupied by pieces. A pawn on d5 would no longer leave d5 very weak!

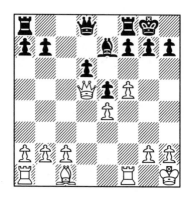

Position after 15.♕xd5

15... **♕c7**

Black wishes to get some relief by either trading queens or putting pressure on the "backward" c-pawn.

16.c4 ...

Another easy move. White makes further inroads to prevent ...d6-d5. He also prepares to activate his bishop and protect his c-pawn with b3.

16... **♕c6**

Still seeking relief.

17.♕xc6 ...

White feels that he has enough advantage (more space, active pieces, a backward pawn to attack) and thus goes into an endgame.

17... **bxc6**
18.♖d1 ...

Again, directed against...d6-d5.

18... **♖ad8**
19.b3 **♖d7**

19...d5?! is a definite possibility. White may play 20.cxd5 cxd5 21.♖xd5 ♖xd5 22.exd5 ♖d8 23.♗e3 with attack on the a-pawn.

20.♗a3 ...

Position after 20.♗a3

More pressure, and more directives against 20...d5!.

20... **♖fd8**

There appears to be nothing better.

21.♖d3 ...

The reasons why White chooses this move:

A) Prepare to double rooks.

B) Put the rook on the relatively clear third rank.

C) Put the rook on a white square so that it won't be bothered later by possible threats from the black bishop.

21...   **g6**

Of course, Black wishes to destroy the white e4-f5 pawn chain.

22.fxg6   **...**

Probably best. 22.g4 g5 closes the kingside off from immediate attention (23.罝ad1 f6).

22...   **hxg6**

Toward the center. On 22...fxg6, White has another open file to seize.

23.g4   **...**

White's umpteenth blockading move. On the "automatic" 23.罝ad1 Black can possibly break out of the bind with 23...f5.

23...   **f5?**

{This is certainly a very strange move. Since Black wishes to counterattack in the center, he might first wish to maneuver his king to e6.}

The losing move. It is natural that Black wishes to open up the center for his pawns to roll, but the weakness of his king will allow White to nicely refute this maneuver.

24.gxf5   **gxf5**

Position after 24...gxf5

25.罝g1+   **...**

{Why check at once? Will the open file run away? On 27.exf5 what would he play?}

A first *Zwischenzug*. White captures the game's first open file.

25...   ♔f7

The only way to roam (Rome?)!

26.exf5   e4

{26...d5 is a more reasonable move if Black doesn't wish to defend himself passively.}

Black expands – into White's hands – not with tempo.

27.♖h3   ...

White threatens to check and double rooks on the seventh.

27...   ♔f6?

{If 27...♖g8 28.♖h7+ ♔f8 29.f6.}

Black wants his pawn back: if he can get it, he doesn't stand so badly. But the text makes it hard for Black to dispute White's control of the open files, so comparatively better is 27...♖g8.

28.♖h5!   ...

Now the threat of 29.♖g6+ ♔e5? 30.f6+ points out Black's woes.

28...   d5?

Opening up White's bishop has fatal consequences. Black's move is nicely refuted by a simple tactical combination.

29.♖g6+   ♔f7

Only!

30.♖h7+   ♔f8

Of course not 30...♔e8?? 31.♖g8+ ♗f8 32.♖xf8#.

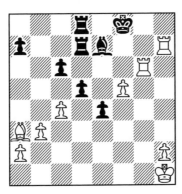

Position after 30...♔f8

31.♖f6+! ...

{What about 31.♗xe7+ ♖xe7 32.♖h8+ ♔f7 33.♖xd8?}

The pin wins. The rest is technique (Ho! Ho!).

31... **♔g8**

Again, if 31...♔e8, 32.♖h8+ and mates.

32.♖xe7 **♖xe7**
33.♗xe7 **♖e8**

Now White's only difficulty is stopping the "unleashed pawns."

34.♖e6 **♔f7**
35.cxd5! ...

The mark of an... "A" player! (Certainly not a master or expert!) If 35...♖xe7 36.♖xe7+ ♔xe7 37.dxc6 is an easy endgame for White.

35... **cxd5**
36.♗c5 ...

A great blockader – with attack on the a-pawn, yet.

36... **♖xe6**
37.fxe6+ **♔xe6**
38.♔g1 **a6**
39.♔f2 **...and soon 1-0**

Go no further! White won. Now let me expound. Although this game is not great, it is of fairly high quality on White's part. And well it may be, because I consider it to be the best 5-minute game I ever played. (How else could I beat Kolker? That's why Kolker did not play the Najdorf.) [And making *Rybka* comments overkill.] Yet the point of this game (= paper) is that White's play was done with only the minimum of thought, yet his play was based almost solely on positional experience. It just goes to show that tactics may just not be 99% of the game – tactics just take up 99% of your time!! {Good point!}

{Ordinarily, I would criticize 13.♘d5, but since Kolker is evidently a very aggressive player, the move makes sense. Black's 23...f5 may be the result of restlessness in a position requiring patience. You might employ that strategy in your next tournament game with him. Swap the pieces and drive him to desperation!}

Game 17

"The Advice of Jim Joachim"

For quite a while now, chess-buddy Jim has been urging ol' Dan to take up the English Opening when playing the white pieces. He feels that it fits my style. Occasionally I give in to this request, more often than not with good results. However, since an expert in an open Swiss-style tournament should have excellent results with White anyhow, I have not been specially swayed to play 1.c4. There are two ways I seem to play the English: the first, because of the English's closed style, is a slow, maneuvering, later breakthrough-style game (à la Heisman – Buchin, 1971 U.S. Team Championship). The other is a sharp tactical battle resulting from the difficulty of simplification in many English lines. The following game is of th e latter, more violent nature.

Dan Heisman (2060) – C. Knight (~1950)
Eastern Open
Washington D.C., 1971
English Opening

1.c4 ...

Now that Bobby plays things other than 1.e4, I don't feel so bad! [A reference to Fischer finally broadening his opening repertoire at the 1971 Interzonal, which he won easily on the way to the 1972 World Championship.]

1... ♘f6

Strangely enough, R.J.Fischer considers this natural reply to be less accurate and flexible than 1...g6, when the black king knight may be developed on e7.

2.♘c3 ...

Penn State's third board and world-class kibitzer Lou Fogg prefers here 2.g3 with the idea of playing against the Bremen System: (2...e5 3.♗g2 c6).

2... g6

This gives White the opportunity to play 3.d4 and allow a Grünfeld

111

or to play the "anti-Grünfeld," 3.e4 which would probably become a King's Indian.

3.g3 ...

I choose to stay in the English.

3... &g7
4.&g2 O-O
5.&f3 (1 minute elapsed) ...

Another good line is 5.e3 with the idea of an eventual &1e2 and d2-d4.

5... c5

This popular line has been a source of mild controversy for some time. If Black wishes to play a ...c7-c5 line, perhaps the knight is better off on e7 as Fischer prefers.

6.O-O &c6
7.&b1 (2) ...

This popular plan (to play b2-b4) I originally picked up from Lou Fogg, but it was originally popularized by former World Champion Vassily Smyslov. This game shows how effective the uninhibited advance can be.

7... d6

Sometimes this is considered a waste of tempo. For instance, in the line 7...a6 8.a3 &b1 9.b4 cxb4 10.axb4 b5 11.cxb5 axb5 12.d4 (better than 12.d3 as in K. Belli-Heisman, 1971) 12...d5 13.&e5! ±. Incidentally, this line shows one of the main ideas behind 7.&b1. It is dangerous, however, to allow this maneuver &a1-b1, a2-a3 and b2-b4 without counterplay, as this game shows.

8.a3 (4) &b8(?)

Too late. Fogg here plays 8...a5, indeed the only logical follow-up to 7...d6.

9.b4 (7) &f5

Black's idea (I guess!?); he wants to develop the bishop with tempo and make White weaken the a1-h8 diagonal for his (Black's) king's bishop.

10.d3 (9) ...

In a situation like this, one should realize that he has no fear of a discovered attack by Black on the knight.

10...   ♞**d7**

Black wishes to occupy e5 – but he soon runs into trouble with this idea.

11.♗d2   ...

Played immediately. The bishop guards the knight, develops pressure along two diagonals, and readies White's queenside action.

11...   ♞**7e5**

Consistent, but dangerous. Black allows White too much leeway on the queenside. [*Rybka* prefers 11...♞d4 ⩲.]

12.♞xe5 (17)   ...

Much of my time spent here was used simply to find how I could best take advantage of the misplaced black pieces in the center.

12...   ♗**xe5**

Forced, as 12...♞xe5 13.bxc5 wins the black b-pawn and, of course, 12...cxb4 loses to 13.♞xc6. White is now in a position to drive away the black bishops with gain of time and space.

13.h3 (23)   ...

The idea behind this move is to make the possibility of a White pawn storm (f2-f4, g3-g4 with the idea of f4-f5) with a great gain in space possible without loss of tempo. 13.e4 would not have accomplished the same end because of the resulting weakness on d4. However, there is a drawback in that White could have played the strong 13.b5 immediately, resulting in lines similar to the game. Black should now take steps to prevent this possibility.

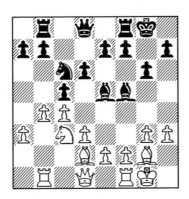

Position after 13.h3

13...   **h5?**

Black actually seems to think that he has the advantage! How else does one explain this "aggressive" sortie? [*R:* better is 13...♕d7.] His pieces do not dominate the center; actually the move played seriously weakens the kingside (as will be seen!) and allows White his thematic thrust:

14.b5 (32)   **...**

Now Black has a problem.

14...   **♘d4**

Black allows a combination. He does not wish to have his knight caught "on the rim." For instance, 14...♘a5 15.♘d5 would threaten 16.♘xe7+, but if 15...e6 then 16.♘e3 with the idea of playing g3-g4, e.g., 16...b6 17.g4 hxg4 18.hxg4 ♕h4? 19.f4. In any event, Black would eventually have to play ...♘a5-b7 and maybe even then ...♘d8 to reactivate his knight – not a very pleasant prospect.

15.e3 (38)   **...**

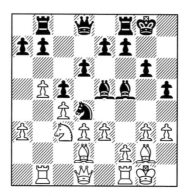

Position after 15.e3

This "loses" two pawns and a rook for a bishop and knight, but White's game will be "um-um good."

15...   **♗xd3**

Black could not play ...♘e6 because of e3-e4 winning a piece, so the text is forced.

16.exd4 (38)   **cxd4**

Also 16...♗xd4 comes into consideration, because if White tries to win Black's "better" king bishop, the following sequence could result:

17.♘e2 ♗xb1 18.♘xd4 ♗d3 19.♘e2 (19.♗h6??) 19...♗xc4 which isn't nearly so bad for Black as the game continuation. However, White can improve with 18.♕xb1 (instead of ♘xd4) and his pieces would quickly dominate the board.

17.♘e2 (45)   ...

I don't know why I took so long to make this obvious move! Just careful, I could say.

17...   **♗xb1**

Or else Black has nothing to show for the piece.

18.♕xb1   ...

Black is "up materially," but White is far better developed and his pieces can quickly control the board. Black is also weak on both the white and black squares around his king, and as one of my friends, Connie Czaplicki, says, "That can't be bad" (for White!). This, of course, is a direct result of the impetuous 13...h5?.

18...   **♕b6**

Black begins to go astray. He understandably wants to hold onto the pawn at d4 and so is reluctant to play ...♗g7 with the idea of ...e7-e5 because he is already behind in development and this would further weaken his central squares. [*R:* 18...♗g7 is best, when White is only slightly better.] With this type of material imbalance (White has more "pieces" but fewer pawns early in the game), if White can quickly establish strong squares for his pieces, he will almost always have a winning game.

19.♘f4 (49)   ...

I could not resist this move – containing a deadly threat which must be met.

19...   **♕c5?**

A terrible blunder in a difficult position. Necessary was either 19...♗xf4, which would give White two strong bishops, or 19...♔g7. In the latter case, I would probably answer with the simple 20.♘d5 with advantage, e.g., 20...♕c5 21.♕d3 e6 22.♗b4.

20.♘xg6 (53)   ...

Of course – this wins.

20...   **fxg6**

Accepting this sacrifice is suicidal – but declining it isn't so hot, either! Black simply has to hope that White will slip up on the attack (which isn't all that trivial) to leave Black with a won game because of his material advantage.

21.♕xg6+   **...**

The first move is easy!

21...   **♗g7**

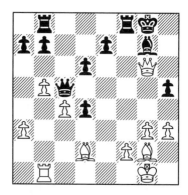

Position after 20...♗g7

Of course not 21...♔h8 22.♕h6+ (22.♕h5+ is O.K., too) 22...♔g8 23.♗d5+ e6 24.♗xe6+ ♖f7 25.♕g6+, etc.

22.♗d5+ (66)   **...**

This move took me 13 minutes. It took me a while to see a certain detail further in the analysis, as will be revealed shortly.

22...   **e6**

Forced – to deflect the bishop off the d5 square. If 22...♔h8? 23.♕xh5+ and *finis*. Originally, I had contemplated now playing 23.♗h6 ♕c7 24.♗xe6+ ♔h8 25.♗f5 ♖xf5 (if 25...♗xh6 26.♕xh6+ ♔g8 27.♗e6+) 26.♗xg7+ ♕xg7 27.♕xf5, but I decided that after 27...♕e5 (really, I saw this – remember, it is *very* forcing and I took 13 minutes on my 22nd move) Black would be able to put up some minimal resistance. During those 13 minutes, it wasn't until I saw a certain facet of the game continuations's 25th move that I realized I had a much stronger line.

23.♗xe6+ (68)   **...**

Returning once again to my original decision; the two minutes were spent just making sure that my "other" analysis decided upon during my 22nd move was O.K.

23...   **♔h8**

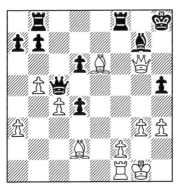

Position after 23...♔h8

24.♗d5!   ...

Played immediately.

24...   **♖f6**

This had been the defense I had originally feared, but...

25.♕h5+   **♗h6**
26.♗xh6   ...

This is what I had originally missed when first analyzing my 22nd move; I didn't realize that my bishop on d2 covered the h6 square in this line. The rest is quick but maybe not painless.

26...   **♕c7**

To stop mate.

27.♗g5+   **♔g7**
28.♗xf6+   **♔xf6**
29.♕h6+   **1-0**

Black is mated: 29...♔e5 (or 29...♔f5 30.g4+ first) 30.♖e1+ and then mate, or 29...♔e7 30.♖e1+ ♔d7 31.♕e6+ ♔d8 32.♕e8#.

Game 18

"Faith in the Center"

I had had a very bad team tournament at the Chicago Pan American Intercollegiate in 1970 [a tournament later immortalized in the wonderful science fiction story "Infinite Variations" by George R.R. Martin], but the Toronto Pan-Am in 1971 was a different story. By far my finest game of the tournament was this game against the Wisconsin first board. The tenth move was the crucial point of the game. I decided to allow my opponent a menacing position, putting my faith in the eventual breakthrough in the center. Like my game with Yehl (#10), the counter-attack came swiftly and decisively.

John Dowling (2060) – Dan Heisman (2100)
Pan American Intercollegiate, Toronto 1971
Queen's Pawn Game

1.d4	♘f6
2.♘f3	...

It is very unusual to play ♘f3 on the second move here. Black now has the possibility of going into a King's Indian or Benoni where White is prevented from playing sharp systems where he advances the f-pawn.

2...	e6

I don't take advantage of the opportunity.

| 3.e3 | ... |

White is actually going to play a Colle System – Black decides to proceed normally against ♘f3 systems by fianchettoing his queen's bishop. This shows the advantage of playing 1...♘f6.

3...	b6
4.♗d3	♗b7
5.♘bd2	c5

Black proceeds logically to undermine White's center.

6.O-O	♗e7
7.dxc5?	...

Incorrect. If White thought that he would wait for Black's king's bishop to move so that this exchange would win a tempo (as Black would wait before capturing on c4 in the Queen's Gambit), then he was badly mistaken.

**7...				bxc5**

Of course this is the correct way to recapture; Black now gets a strong potential center.

**8.♖e1				...**

White bases his play on getting in e4, which would also be playable immediately.

**8...				♘c6**

Now 9.e4 would be met not by 9...♘b4 10.e5 ♘xd3 11.cxd3 (11.exf6? ♘xe1 12.fxe7 ♘f3+) 11...♘d5 12.♘c4 ±, but by 9...d5 when 10.exd5 exd5 11.c4?! ♘b4?! 12.♗f5 O-O 13.a3 = might be a continuation.

**9.c3				...**

To stop ...♘c6-b4 in some lines.

**9...				O-O**

This continuation is interesting. The alternative, 9...d5, was rejected because I thought that White would have two break-moves in the center against the d5 square, e3-e4 and c3-c4. Indeed, though, Black would be *one tempo ahead* because of White's 9.c3 and there should be no reason why a one-move thrust of 9...d5 wouldn't work. It does seem Black has reasonable lines because his pieces are well placed.

**10.e4				...**

Of course. 11.e5 is now probably a threat. What is Black to do against this maneuver? White can then continue with moves like ♘c4 and ♗f4 with an excellent game.

**10...				d5!**

Before looking at ...d7-d5, let's consider some of the alternatives:

A) 10...d6 11.e5 dxe5 12.♘xe5 ♘xe5 13.♖xe5 ♗d6(!) similar to a later theme in the game. However, after 10...d6, 11.♘c4 looks playable.

B) 10...♘g4?! and

B1) 11.e5 d6 is unclear, and
B2) 11.♘c4 d5 12.exd5 exd5 13.♘4e5 ♘4xe5 14.♘xe5 ♘xe5 15.♖xe5 ♗d6, and if 16.♖h5, then 16...g6 seems playable with the idea of ...c5-c4(?) or ...♕f6.

I based my hope on 10...d5 almost purely on a positional basis. Since 11.e5 ♘d7 12.♗xh7+ is ridiculous, Black will have achieved a pawn formation in the center similar to that of the French Defense, with the exception that the all-important white d-pawn is missing. This will leave the e-pawn weak and give Black control of the c4-d4-e4 squares. With the d-pawn free to advance, Black has a potentially powerful game if he can wrest the initiative. I'll let the reader judge the results for himself.

11.e5   ...

Interesting is 11.exd5 exd5 12.c4?! d4 13.♘e4 when White's pieces have more potential than in the game; however, I can see why my opponent is reluctant to allow me the powerful passed pawn on d4. Maybe he should immediately try to undermine my center at that point with the thematic b2-b4 break.

11...   ♘d7

Position after 11...♘d7

11...♘e8 not only puts less pressure on e5, but makes ...f7-f6 difficult. Also, from d7, the knight can go to f8, making an attack on h7 difficult.

12.♘f1   ...

White has intentions of a kingside attack; he wishes to have his queen's knight and bishop participate. Better is 12.c4, making Black make some commitment in the center.

12...   ♖e8

Not as mysterious as it looks. Black wishes to break with ...f7-f6, and to recapture after exf6 with the bishop. This move ensures the protection of the e-pawn and also clears f8 for the knight.

13.h3? ...

White is unaware of the danger. He dreams of a kingside attack where Black is so unable to find counterplay that White can simply maneuver ♘d2-f1-h2-g4 △ ♘h6 or ♘f6. This would be nice if the center were closed, but...

13... **f6**

What did White expect? Now 14.exf6 ♗xf6 gives Black a great game. [*R:* Better is 13...♕b6 or 13...♕c7.]

14.♕c2 ...

Still hoping for a kingside attack. [*R:* 14.exf6 =.]

14... **♘f8**

All according to plan. Black need make only this one defensive move and White has nothing.

15.♘h2 ...

Continuing with the faulty plan. It was much better to play 15.♗f4 (or 15.exf6 with the idea of ♗f4) and wait and see whether the knight belonged on d2, e3 or g3. [*R:* 15.exf6 with a tiny edge.]

15... **c4**

[*Rybka* proposes15...f5 with a tiny edge to Black.]

16.♗f1 **fxe5**

I thought for a while before this capture. It was not immediately apparent to me how strong my plan was. But I kept looking until I found something to my liking because I could feel something was there! [Making use of one of Steinitz's rules: If your evaluation of the static position shows you have the advantage, then there must be a dynamic continuation that preserves the advantage; else there is something faulty in your evaluation process, for a static advantage must be realizable!]

17.♘xe5 ...

Forced.

17... **♘xe5**
18.♖xe5 **♗d6**

Black's plan is taking shape. He is ready to dominate the center. His 15th move, ...c5-c4, which forced the bishop away from the light squares in the center, works harmoniously with the present maneuver to command the dark squares.

[According to *Rybka* the position is roughly equal. White should play b2-b3 in the near future to break up Black's central pawn dominance.]

19.♖e1 ...

For the first time White perceives the danger. The move 19.♖h5, more in tune with White's previous moves, is now seen to be completely out of place, since the rook is open to attack and White realizes that he is no longer has the initiative. [*R:* I like 19.♖h5 better!]

19... ♘g6

Black no longer has to worry about White's control of h7, so he grabs control of e5 and f4.

20.♘f3 ...

White sees that his original plan, to play ♘e5-g4, is now useless and so develops his knight on a more useful square. ♖emember, this knight has now made the maneuver ♘d2-f1-h2-f3!

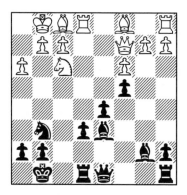

Position after 20.♘f3

20... ♕d7!

[One of my all-time favorite moves. I remember at the time I distinctly "felt" ...♕d7 was not only the right move, but one of my best, and I was right.] Black's advantage is tangible. This simple but strong queen move demonstrates the strength of his position: He has two unopposed, and thus mobile, center pawns; his bishops aim at the white king; his rooks are connected and white's king's bishop is back on its original square. [*R:* Nevertheless, 20...e5 is better.] No wonder White gets impatient and plays...

21.h4? ...

An attack which is premature or unjustified. If your opponent has the advantage, then theoretically an attack is doomed to failure. Better was simply 21.♗g5. White now threatens 22.♘g5 △ ♘xh7 and h4-h5. Black, however, sees further and plays...

21...   **e5**

The way to activate the two bishops in this case is to block both of them with black pawns! For after these pawns advance with threats (and advances are unstoppable), the bishops will rule the position. If now 22.♘g5? ♕g4!. Thanks to 19...♕d7!. I didn't see this future use for the queen, but the general attack on certain light squares helped me to decide on the important d7 square.

22.h5   **...**

Consistent, but meets a drastic counter.

22...   **e4!**

Of course! Despite the two pawns on light squares, the light-squared black bishop will be devastating on the diagonal. I reveled in the rare chance to "sac" two pawns for the forthcoming attack.

23.hxg6   **...**

Other moves are no better:

A) 23.♘g5 ♘f4 and if 24.♗xf4 ♗xf4 25.♘h3 ♗h6 and Black shuts out White's pieces.

B) 23.♘d4 ♘f4 (or 23...♘e5 △ ♘d3). Note how White's knight is stymied by the powerful queen. [*R:* Best is 23.♘d4 ♘e5 when Black is on the verge of winning.]

C) 23.♘h2 ♘f4 as above.

23...   **exf3**
24.gxh7+   **...**

Why not? [*Rybka* says White is lost; relatively best is 24.♖xe8+.]

24...   **♔h8**

Other moves (tongue in cheek) are weaker.

25.♖xe8+(?)   **...**

This move is unreasonable. It cedes the file to Black and makes White's task difficult, if not impossible. Bad also is 25.♗g5 when, after the reply 25...♕g4, it can be seen that White will lose a vital tempo. Also, 25.♗e3 will allow a vital tempo ...d5-d4 later in some lines. 25.♗d2 is better, but it cuts off the queen from the defense.

25...   **♖xe8**

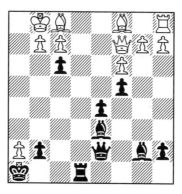

Position after 25...罩xe8

26.gxf3?! ...

A key move in the game. This is one of the toughest positions I've ever had to analyze! Does Black have a *forced* win after *any* White reply? [In other words, had White already made the losing move or is it 26.gxf3?! – *R:* it was made earlier.]

The two most reasonable moves for White are A) 26.豐g6 and B) 26.臭e3:

A) After 26.豐g6, 26...罩e6 seems unreasonable because of 27.豐f5; so Black's best appears to be 26...罩e1, reaching an interesting position. White can try 27.b3 (to free both bishops) and then Black could try either

A1) 27...臭f4 (27...臭a3? 28.臭b2) so to keep both bishops locked after 28.臭b2 (28.臭xf4?!), or

A2) Sharper seems to be 27...fxg2 28.豐xg2 (28.曲xg2?!) 28...d4 29.f3 with wild complications, e.g., 29...臭f4!? 30.臭b2 (30.臭xf4 罩xa1 and Black should win) 30...臭e3+ 31.曲h1 (31.曲h2? 豐d6+) 31...罩xa1 32.臭xa1 豐f5 33.臭e2 (33.曲h2 臭xf3 34.豐h3 豐e5+ 35.豐g3 臭f4–+) 33...d3 34.臭d1 豐h5+ 35.豐h2 豐xf3+ 36.臭xf3 臭xf3+:

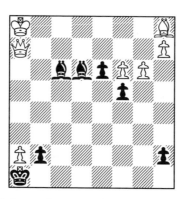

Position after 36...臭xf3+ (analysis)

37.♕g2 ♗xg2+ 38.♔xg2 d2 and the pawn queens.

B) Also leading to some very pretty sacrificial lines is the reply 26.♗e3, with the purpose of developing the bishop to aim at the weak dark squares (to possibly get in ♗d4) and to release his own rook while preventing ...♖e8-e1. One strong line for Black is 26...♕g4 27.♖d1 (if 27.♗d4, then after 27...♕h5 28.g3 ♖e6 {△ ♖h6} if White plays 29.♗e3 {what else?} to prevent ...♖e6-h6 and ...♕h5-h1 mate, he will enter lines similar to the following variations one or two tempi down due to the loss of time taken for ♗d4-e6 {also, on 27.g3, at a minimum, Black has 27... ♗xg3 28.fxg3 ♕xg3+ 29.♔h1 ♖xe3}) 27...♕h5 28.g3:

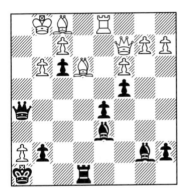

Position after 28.g3 (analysis)

28...d4! (Much better than 28...♗xg3; 29.fxg3 ♖xe3 30.♕h2 and the white queen's defense allows the game to continue for a while longer. Remember what was said earlier about opening lines for this bishop!) and Black wins:

    B1) 29.♖xd4 ♗xg3 30.fxg3 (30.♗xc4 is mated after ...♕h2+) 30...f2+ 31.♔xf2 (forced or else mate) 31...♕h2+ 32.♔e1 ♕xc2.

    B2) 29.♗xd4 ♗xg3 30.♗xg7+ (29.fxg3 is as in line 1) 30...♔xg7 31.♖d7+ ♔h8 and White is helpless, as above.

    B3) 29.cxd4 ♗xg3 as above.

    B4) 29.♗f4 (other moves allow ...♗xg3) 29...♗xf4 30.gxf4 (most other moves allow 30...♗xg3 or remain a piece down with no compensation) 30...♕g4+ 31.♔h2 ♖e6 and White has no adequate defense against 32... ♖h6+ 33.♗h3 ♖xh3#, e.g., 32.♗h3 ♖h6.

These lines seem to indicate that White's position is grave after moves other than 26.gxf3?!. Moves other than 26.♗e3 or 26.♕g6 are also possible, but all seem to lead to similar, dangerous Black attacks. [Conclusion: 26.gxf3 is not the losing move; it was probably 25.♖xe8.] 26.gxf3?! itself looks terrible, but in what way is Black able to force a quick win?

26...   ♖e1(!)

Must be best. No use examining other lines.

27.♕g6   ...

Too late! The only other move worth considering, and I was very fearful of it at the time, was 27.♔h2. However, after the game I realized that this seemingly strong defensive move is easily defeated by the reply 27...♗c8! [An uncanny similarity to the rare mating pattern of ♗c8/♕d7 shown in Game 14, note A1 to move 21!] forcing 28.♔g1 ♕h3 and mates.

27...   ♕h3

With many mate threats: ...♕h2, ...♖xf1, ...♕xf1.

28.♕e8+   ...

Cute but desperate. White realizes that the logical defensive move fails: 28.♕g2 ♗h2+ 29.♔h1 (29.♕xh2 ♖xf1#) 29...♖xf1+ 30.♕xf1 ♕xf1+ 31.♔xh2 ♕xf2+ −+. White now hopes to delay the game after 28...♖xe8? 29.♗xh3, but after 29...♖e1+ 30.(any) ♗f4 Black wins the exchange and undoubtedly the game anyhow.

28...   ♔xh7
0-1

Mate is unavoidable: e.g., 29.♕xe1 ♕h2#. Because my opponent played better than Yehl (Game #10), maybe *this* is my best game. Certainly the games against Yehl, Latzel (#14), and this one against Dowling led to some interesting tactical combinations and positions, both in the games and the notes.

Snippet #1

What is the best puzzle I have ever solved over the board? I'll nominate the following, which occurred in R. Anderson – Heisman, Continental Intercollegiate, New York 1970: 1.e4 c5 2.♘f3 d6 3.d4 cxd4 4.♘xd4 ♘f6 5.♘c3 a6 6.♗g5 e6 7.f4 ♗e7 8.♕f3 ♕c7 9.0-0-0 ♘bd7 10.g4 b5 11.♗xf6 ♘xf6 12.g5 ♘d7 13.f5 ♘c5 14.f6 15.gxf6 gxf6 ♗f8 16.♗h3 b4 17.♘d5 exd5 18.exd5 ♗xh3 19.♖he1+ ♔d8 20.♘c6+ ♔c8 21.♕xh3+ ♕d7 22.♕h4 a5 23.♖e2 ♔c7 24.♖de1 ♕f5? (In 1988's *Najdorf for the Tournament Player*, GM Nunn says that 24...♔b6 25.♔b1 ♖g8 defends) 25.♕c4 ♔b6 26.♘d4:

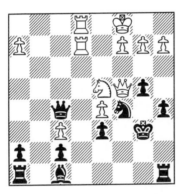

Position after 26.♘d4

Black is up a piece but is paying dearly for his one transgression. White threatens 27.♕b5+ and a quick mate after 28.♖e7+. How can Black defend? If 26...♕d7, then after 27.♖e7 ♗xe7 28.♖xe7 ♕a4 29.b3 forces Black's queen off the a4-e8 diagonal and White either wins the queen or mates after ♕b5+. Can Black save the game? Turn the page for the answer.

I thought for 18 minutes and played 26...♕d7, admitting my mistake. White saw nothing better than to proceed with the line on the previous page: 27.♖e7 ♗xe7 28.♖xe7 ♕a4 29.b3, but I had foreseen that at this point I actually have a continuation that allows me not to resign: 29... ♘xb3+!:

Position after 29...♘xb3+

Despite the fact that White has four ways to recapture his piece, Black stays alive in all lines:

A) 30.axb3 ♕a1+ 31.♔d2 ♕c3+ 32.♕xc3 bxc3+ 33.♔xc3, and while White is probably somewhat better despite being a pawn down for the exchange, the game is no more over than it is in the line that was actually played.

B) 30.cxb3! ♖ac8 (30...♖hc8 is less accurate) 31.♘c6 ♖xc6 (after 31...♕a3+ 32.♔b1 White's attack will win; 31...♕b5?? loses to 32.♖b7+) 32.dxc6 ♕xc6 33.♕xc6+ ♔xc6 34.♖xf7 ± is White's best line (analysis by *Zarkov*).

C) 30.♕xb3 ♕xb3, and "Black is O.K."

D) The game continuation: 30.♘xb3 ♖hc8 31.♕d4+ ♔a6 32.♔b1 ♕b5 33.♖xf7 ♕e2 34.♕d3+ (I can breathe a little easier) 34...♕xd3 35.cxd3 ♖f8 36.♖xh7 ♖xf6 37.♘d4 ♖f2 38.♖d7 ♔b6! 39.♘e6 ♖g8! −+ 40.♖xd6+ ♔b5 41.♖c6 ♖g1+ 42.♖c1 ♖xc1+ 43.♔xc1 ♖xh2 (I can breathe quite a bit easier) 44.♔b1 ♖d2 45.d4 ♔b6! (waiting; White is in *Zugzwang*) 46.♔a1 a4 47.♔b1 a3 (total *Zugzwang*) 48.♔a1? (hastening the end in a clearly lost position) 48...♖d1#.

It was games like this that caused me to give up the Najdorf as my full-time defense to 1.e4. Too many players rated under 2000 know this kind of book for 25+ moves. I'd rather take the chance the game might even end by then if I play something different! Also, not playing the latest sharp lines means less studying and not having to keep up with the newest innovations.

Game 19

I Become an Expert

M y rating reached 1900 after two years of play. However, in my first several games where a particular result would have made me an expert, I failed. Finally, just before my sophomore season (in the same tournament as Games #11 and #13), I made the breakthrough, and against a worthy opponent. John, now "Jack," Peters was one of New England's up-and-coming superstars. Now an established IM and a fixture in the Southern California chess media, Peters was even then a formidable opponent. I was about a year older, 19 to 18, but he was already an expert (remember, then the ratings were lower; today a player like Peters would have already easily made master). John, as he signed my scoresheet, was a very approachable and memorable opponent.

John Peters (2100) – Dan Heisman (1950)
Merrimac Grand Prix, New Hampshire 1969
Sicilian Defense
(50 moves in 2 hours)

1.e4	c5
2.♘f3	d6
3.d4	cxd4
4.♘xd4	♘f6
5.♘c3	a6

Najdorf again.

6. f4 ...

The f4 variation, thanks to the British theoreticians, was then gaining in popularity. Luckily for me, it was not until a little later that I learned about the tricky and trappy main defense involving Black's fianchettoing his king bishop. I happily improvised.

6...	♕c7
7.♗d3	e5
8.♘f3	b5
9.O-O	♗e7

I permanently give up any idea of fianchettoing this bishop. Peters knew that the correct idea for White if Black doesn't fianchetto is to exchange on e5 and then play ♘h4-f5 with a good position. Today theory recommends that Black postpone ...♗e7 to keep things going on the queenside with ...♘bd7 and/or ...♗b7.

10.♕e1   **...**

The thematic switch of the queen to the kingside to participate in an attack there.

10...   **♗b7**

Sometimes in positions like these it is better for Black first to try 10...b4. Play could continue 11.♘d5?! or 11.♘b1 a5 12.c3, when often Black's pawns become too advanced.

11.a3	**♘bd7**
12.♔h1	**O-O** (7)
13.fxe5	**dxe5** (11)
14.♗g5	**♖fe8** (16)
15.♕g3	**♗f8** (29)
16.♘h4	**...**

Continuing with the correct plan, as explained earlier. Black's passive play has already given White a dangerous kingside attack.

16...	**♔h8** (36)
17.♘f5	**♘g8** (44)

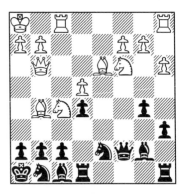

Position after 17...♘g8

It would be kind to call this a "Steinitz" defense, in deference to the great World Champion who didn't mind retreating.

[*R:* Better is 17...♘h5 to avoid the sacrifice White missed on the next move. After 17...♘h5 18.♕g4 ♘f4 19.♘e3, White would have a "normal" small opening advantage.]

18.♘d5 ...

This gives Black a chance to do something. Bringing the queen's rook into play, say after 18.♖f3 with 19.♖1f1, looks good. In giving this position to *Zarkov*, it thinks White has a pawn advantage, which seems about right. It also thinks White holds the advantage at this level until about move 27.

[According to *Rybka*, White misses the clever breakthrough 18.♘xg7!! ♗xg7 19.♖xf7:

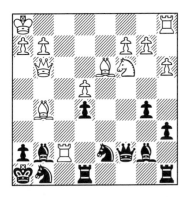

Position after 19.♖xf7 (analysis)

Black must play 19...♕c6 but after 20.♘d5 Black is forced to abandon his knight on d7 with 20...♕g6 21.♖xd7 with a winning position. If instead Black tries to continue guarding his knight with 20...♖ac8, then 21.♖xg7! ♔xg7 22.♗f6+ ♔f7 23.♕g7+ ♔e6 24.♗h4 ♘c5 25.♖d1! with a decisive attack.]

18...	**♗xd5** (53)
19.exd5	**g6** (54)

A weakening, but Black will regain some space.

| **20.♘d4** | **♘c5** (70) |

[*R:* Better is 20...♘b6 =.]

| **21.♘c6** | **♘xd3** (78) |

[*R:* Don't like this move at all. Better is 21...♗g7 or 21...f5.]

22.cxd3 ...

[*Rybka* notes that the natural 22.♕xd3 leaves White with a nice advantage.]

22...   **f5** (82)

[*R:* Again inaccurate. Much better is 22...♕d6 or 22...♗g7.]

23.d4   ♕**d6** (88)
24.dxe5   ♕**xd5**
25.♖ac1   ♕**e6** (93)

I have less than half an hour left for 25 moves! When I analyzed this game with *Zarkov*, around this point it wanted to play ...♖ac8, but I wanted to shore up my weakened kingside first.

26.♖c2   **...**

[*R:* 26.♖fd1 is better, with a nice advantage to White.]

26...   ♗**g7** (96)
27.♗f4   ♘**e7** (101)
28.♖1c1   ♘**d5** (103)

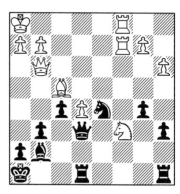

Position after 28...♘d5

Black's pieces begin to come out of their hibernation. Steinitz would be proud. *Zarkov* suggested an interesting simplification which I did not consider: 28...♖ac8 29.♘xe7 ♖xc2 30.♘xg6+ ♕xg6 31.♖xc2 ♕xg3 32.♗xg3 ♗xe5 33.♗xe5 ♖xe5, but after 34.♔g1 White would have definite winning possibilities with multiple weak black pawns. Of course, in this position Peters wanted more than a better endgame.

29.♖c5   **...**

The immediate 29.♘d4 allows Black to play 29...♕e7 when White doesn't have anything much better than to repeat the position with 30.♘c6.

29...   **♗f8** (106)

Less than 15 minutes left for me. I recall that White didn't have much more. *Zarkov* suggests I might consider getting rid of the bishop with 29...♘xf4 30.♕xf4 ♖ac8 31.♘d4? ♕d7(?). I didn't like the looks of 32.d6, but *Zarkov* said I would have had the shot 31...♖xc5! (instead of 31...♕d7) when after 32.♘xe6 ♖xe5 White cannot move his Knight due to the mate threat and when the smoke clears Black's free and easy game, along with the rook, bishop, and pawn for queen give him the advantage. White could retain his advantage with 31.b4! instead of 31.♘d4.

[*R*: 29...♗f8 is fine and Black is fully equal.]

30.♘d4   **♕g8**
31.♖c6   **♗g7** (110)
32.e6?   **...**

This aggressive push is actually a mistake. White can retain his advantage with 32.♘f3 after, for example, 32...♘xf4 33.♕xf4 ♖ac8 34.♖c7 ♖xc7 35.♖xc7. Now the e-pawn becomes weak.

[*R*: 32.♘f3 is best, but the position is equal after 32...♘xf4 33.♕xf4 ♕d5.]

32...   **♘xf4(!)**

This is much better than 32...♗xd4 33.♗e5+ ♗xe5 34.♕xe5+ ♕g7 35.♕xd5 ♕xb2 36.♖c7, when Black has to defend carefully with either 36...♖a7!? 37.♕c6 ♖e7 or 36...♖ad8 37.♕b7 ♖e7!. Instead 32...♘xf4 wins the dangerous e-pawn.

33.♕xf4

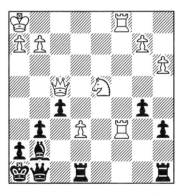

Position after 33.♕xf4

33...   **♖ad8** (113)

A key move. On the previous move 32...♗xd4 followed by ...♖xe6 was no threat because White could recapture on d4 with check. Now the queen recapture is no longer possible, so White loses his precious e-pawn and the advantage. I only have seven minutes for the next 17 moves, so it is still not going to be easy for Black!

34.♘f3   **♖xe6**
35.♖c7   **♖e4**

If I had played this game when I got older, I never would have been able to keep up with the threats. A 19-year-old is much faster!

36.♕g3   **♖8e8** (115)

This move starts an unintentional comedy of errors. Both players feel the b-pawn is poison due to White's threats. However, for many of the moves until I actually capture the pawn on move 42, *Zarkov* indicates that ...♗xb2 is the best move, as it does here (and correspondingly thinks White should guard it with a move like ♕b4). For example, the computer gave the following fantastic line which turns White's seemingly threatening position into mush: 36...♗xb2 37.♘g5 ♖c4!! (*not* stopping 38.♘f7+; 37...♗e5 and 37...♗xc1 also are good, but not quite as forcing) 38.♖b1 (doesn't work, but it is about the only White try to give Black a problem; after 38.♖7xc4 ♕xc4 39.♖e1 White is just down two pawns. Of course, after 38.♘f7+?? ♕xf7 wins on the spot) 38...f4!:

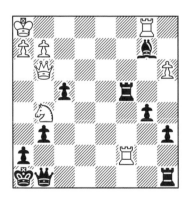

Position after 38...f4! (analysis)

when Black's threats far outshine White's, e.g.,

A) 39.♕b3 ♖xc1+ wins the queen, or

B) 39.♕h4 ♖xc7 wins the rook!

C) 39.♘f7+ ♕xf7 and Black wins a piece due to the weak back rank: 40.♖xf7 fxg3 41.♖xb2?? ♖c1, mating.

I am sure I would have seen this if not in time trouble (ha ha).

37.♘g5   **♖4e7**

The simplification 37...♗e5! was better, e.g., 38.♘f7+ (other moves just lose the c7 Rook) 38...♕xf7 39.♖xf7 ♗xg3 40.♕xg3 ♖e1+ 41.♖xe1 ♖xe1+ 42.♔h2 ♖e2 when Black has good winning chances.

38.♖xe7   **♖xe7**

Somewhere around this point or a little before, I made my move and said, "In my little time left, I offer you a draw!" Peters surveyed the situation, made his move quickly and said very cordially, "In my little time left, I decline!" I'll never forget that exchange of civilities in the midst of a complicated time struggle.

39.♕d6   **...**

If 39.b4, then 39...♗e5 40.♕h4 ♖d7 gives Black a comfortable game. In time trouble, Peters's move is much harder to meet.

39...   **♕e8**

In time trouble, mate threats take on added psychological and practical significance...

40.♘f3   **...**

...such as causing the attacking army to retreat! *Zarkov* again suggests 40.♕b4, holding both b2 and e1, for if 40...♗xb2??? trying to distract the queen from e1, then 41.♕xb2 is check!

40...   **♖e3**

Zarkov suggests 40...♗xb2, and if 41.♖d1 then 41...♖e6 when it feels Black is up by well over 2 pawns.

41.♕c7   **...**

Again, *Zarkov* suggests 41.♕b4 or ♕d2 holding the b-pawn.

[*R*: 41.♕xa6! is much better, and equal.]

41...   **♖e2?**

Not until computer analysis was I aware of this double blunder (41...♖e2? and 42.♕b6?). Black throws away all his advantage with this seemingly natural move. The best (only?) way to win is by taking the pawn: 41...♗xb2 42.♖d1 ♖c3 and Black is on his way.

42.♕b6?　　　　　**...**

The wrong square! White can threaten the a-pawn and the queen with the better 42.♕b7! when he has some real chances:

A) 42...♕f8?! 43.b4 ♕f6 44.♕a8+ ♗f8 45.♖c6 =, e.g., 45...♕a1+? 46.♘g1 ♔g7 47.♕xa6.

B) 42...♕g8 43.♕xa6 ♗xb2 44.♖c7 ♖e6 45.♕xb5 ♗xa3 and the reduced material helps White.

42...　　　　　**♗xb2!**

Finally! Incidentally, this bishop move does more than just win a pawn. It asks White the question, "Do you want to defend (the back rank) or do you want to attack?" Peters chose to attack.

43.♖c7　　　　　**♗g7**
44.♕xa6??　　　　　**...**

Allows the nice mate, but by now Black has won a second pawn and is on his way to winning. If 44.♕a7, then 44...♖e6, and on 44.♖b7 ♖c2 45.♕a7 Black can keep his winning advantage with:

A) 45...♖c1+ 46.♘g1 ♕e6 when 47.♖xg7? allows ♖xg1+, or

B) 45...h6.

44...　　　　　**♖e1+**
45.♘g1　　　　　**♖xg1+**
0-1

I remember slumping back in my chair, exhausted by the fight. I had completely forgotten that I needed this win to finally surpass the magic 2000 barrier. Friends Lester Shelton and Ken Boehm came over, incredulous and happy at my victory. I started to speak to them when all of a sudden I remembered. I stopped whatever I had been discussing, beamed widely, and spoke with the kind of pride you can best share with your chess friends: "I'm an Expert!!"

"Choosing an Opening Strategy"

When preparing against an opponent with a known opening system, a player can take one of the following three approaches:

A) "Out-book" your opponent: either know the main lines better than he, or come up with a new move yourself in your home laboratory.

B) Play a rare sideline in the opening, hoping that your opponent won't know it.

C) Avoid a particular opening entirely.

Most amateur chessplayers find "A" to be hard work. Some choose "C," but they themselves must learn something about the opening they choose as the substitute.

In this game, I chose path "B." When playing against the crucial Marshall Attack in the Ruy López, I played a line called the "Thomas Emory" variation, which I started playing after seeing an article about it in *Chess Review*. Did my strategy work? Well, partly...

Dan Heisman (2060) – Peter J. Tamburro, Jr. (1900)
Continental Intercollegiate, New York 1969
Ruy López

1.e4	e5
2.♘f3	♘c6
3.♗b5	a6
4.♗a4	♘f6
5.O-O	♗e7
6.♖e1	b5
7.♗b3	O-O
8.c3	d5

This is the signal for the Marshall Attack. Black offers a pawn for a strong initiative.

9.d4	...

This is the Thomas Emory variation. Many of my opponents felt uncomfortable in this line – a good reason for playing it!

9...   **♗g4**

In the *Chess Review* article, the author, Al Horowitz, said 9...♗g4 was the weakest line, and so I happily and blindly followed his advice. What I didn't know was that I was transposing into a line of the better known "Kevitz" variation, and that I didn't know so much about this line after all!

10.exd5   **e4**
11.dxc6   **exf3**
12.h3(?)   **...**

This is what Horowitz's article had recommended. Unfortunately for me, the best move in this position is currently held to be 12.gxf3, seemingly opening up his own king to attack, but His Majesty will soon have help, e.g. 12.gxf3 ♗h5 13.♗f4 ♗d6 14.♗e5 ♕c8 15.♘d2 ♕h3 16.♖e3 ♖ad8 17.♕f1 ♕f5 18.♕g2 h6!? 19.♖c1! (GM John Nunn in *The Marshall Attack*, 2nd edition, 1988).

[*R:* 12.h3 seems best and does not deserve a question mark, even a muted one in parentheses. It may deserve an exclamation point!]

12...   **♗h5**
13.g4   **♘xg4!**

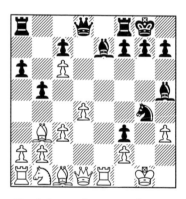

Position after 13...♘xg4!

Horowitz's article had just given the submissive 13...♗g6(?), with a significant advantage for White. But 13...♘xg4! is fully recognized with its exclamation point in Wade and Harding's *The Marshall Attack*, 1st edition, 1974, and they give my reply...

14.hxg4 ...

...a "!?", saying that 14.♕xf3 is safer. My opponent also considered this game worthy of publication. In the October 1973 edition of New Jersey's State Chess Magazine, *Atlantic Chess News*, he surveyed the opening, gave 14.♕xf3 an "!", and included these witty and perceptive remarks about my 14th move:

> In the 1969 U.S. Intercollegiate, Dan Heisman of PA played 14.hxg4 against me. I did not know of the *Chess Review* article at the time and of course had never seen 9.d4 – which led me to wonder what was going on here. Thus, Heisman knew that I had chosen the lamest variation, but he was as confused as the nitwit across the board from him, since Horowitz never analyzed that line.

Since Nunn, considered perhaps the world's leading authority on the Marshall Attack, doesn't even consider 14.♕xf3, quoting only the Zilberstein – Philippe game (see note to White's move 15), we must assume that a major opening error is not 14.hxg4, but White's 15th move.

[*Rybka* deems 14.hxg4 best.]

14... ♗xg4
15.♗f4 ...

Years later, the move 15.♕d2! was discovered and is the key move to the entire variation starting with 12.h3. The idea is that if 15...♗d6, then 16.♕g5 and if 15...h6 16.♕f4, which gave White an overwhelming game in Zilberstein – Philippe, European Club Championship Final 1974. [Note – although in this example it is not a mating attack – the similarity of the ♗c1/♕d2 maneuver here to Game 14, note A1 to move 21 and Game 18, note to move 27. It's really quite a coincidence: all three times the same "Queen on second rank backed on the diagonal by a bishop on first rank" pattern, each not played in the actual game but absolutely crucial to the game's annotation!]

[*R:* 15.♕d2 is indeed best and White is winning.]

15... ♗d6
16.♗xd6 ♕xd6

In the postal game Feller – Glausius, 1971, 16...♕h4 won quickly after White played the erroneous 17.♕d3?, but correct for White is 17.♖e4! cxd6 18.♕xf3 h5 19.♘d2.

17.♘d2 ...

Here we, unbeknownst to us, finally depart from "the 1974 book" – which, of course, had not yet been written! The continuation given in Wade and Harding was 17.♕d3 ♕h6 18.♘d2 ♕h3 19.♕f1 ♕h5 (remember this pattern!) 20.♘e4 ♖ad8! "with an attack." Now, with 17.♘d2, I meet 17...♕g6 with 18.♘e4 ♕h5 19.♖e3 ♕h3 20.♕f1. But I have other problems.

[*Rybka* rates 17.♘d2 as best and White still has the advantage.]

17...   **♖ae8(!)**

Stopping my planned defense to ...♕g6.

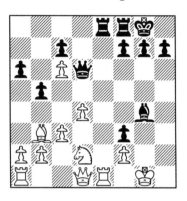

Position after 17...♖ae8

18.♗c2   **...**

Played to stop 18...♕g6, but now the black f-pawn is unpinned. Of course, not 18.♘xf3?? ♖xe1+ −+; and also 18.♖xe8 ♖xe8 19.♘xf3 is met by 19...♕g6 20.♗xf7+?! ♕xf7 21.♘e5 ♖xe5! 22.♕xg4 ♖e6, offering White little positive chances, but in view of the continuation in the game which could have happened (see note to Black's move 22), maybe this was my best chance for salvation!

[*R:* 18.♗c2 is probably a losing move; afterwards Black is much better. 18.♖xe8 ♖xe8 19.♘f1! seems to retain good winning chances for White. It's better to be a computer to play positions like these!]

18...   **♕h6**
19.♖xe8   **♖xe8**
20.♘e4   **...**

Not 20.♘f1? ♕h3 21.♘e3 ♖xe3−+.

20...   **f5**

I was offering Black his piece back by 20...♗f5 21.♕xf3 ♕g6+ and 22...♗xe4, but either Black misses this or is after bigger game.

[*R:* Both 20.♘e4 and 20...f5 were best and Black is still likely winning.]

21.♘g3 ...

[*R*: 21.♕c1 f4! wins, so nothing saves the game.]

21... **f4**
22.♘e4 **♖e6(?)**

At the time I thought this was a strong move, but later my opponent pointed out a clever win by 22...♕h3! 23.♕f1 ♕h5!:

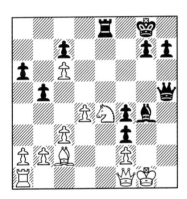

Position after 23...♕h5! (analysis)

The point: he wins a crucial tempo to overprotect his f-pawn with a maneuver similar to the one shown in the note after White's 17th move. Black has the unstoppable threat of 24...♗h3, threatening both 25... ♕g6+ as well as 25...♗g2 followed by 26...♕h1#. Having missed this, things "settle down" – a little.

[*R*: 22...♖e6?. Instead 22...♕g6, 22...♕h5, and 22...♕h3 all win.]

23.♗b3 ...

[*R*: White makes the most of his chance. 23.♗b3 is best by far, not that it is a difficult move to find.]

23... **♕g6**

[In *Rybka's* view, better is 23...♕h3 =.]

24.♘g3 □ ...

The only defense. Not 24.♗xe6+ (a rare case where winning material with check is bad!) 24...♗xe6+ (two straight checking moves with the same notation is rare, also!) 25.♔f1 ♕xe4! (but not 25...♗h3+ 26. ♔e1 ♕xe4+ 27.♔d2 and White escapes) 26.♕b1 (to cover g6) 26...♗h3+ 27.♔g1 ♕e6 28.♔h2 ♗g2 and Black mates.

141

[*R:* 24.♘g3 is best, but not the only defense. White can also play 24.♕e1 or 24.♗d5.]

24...	**fxg3**
25.♗xe6+	**♗xe6**
26.♕xf3	**gxf2+**
27.♔f2	**♕c2+**
28.♔g1	**♕g6+**

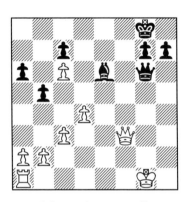

Position after 28...♕g6+

29.♔f2   ...

[*R:* Much better is 29.♕g2, with winning chances.]

29...	**♕c2+**
30.♕e2	**♕f5+**
31.♔e1	**♕g6**
½-½	

Can either side play for a win? We sure didn't think so!

[*R:* I think so! White can try 32.b3 or 32.♕e5 with some advantage.]

Game 21

Taking the Calculated Risk

There are two noteworthy lessons in this game.

One is that most games reach crucial points, and it is at these key points where the superior player usually asserts himself.

The second lesson is that the objectively best move is not always the move that, in practice, generates the best chance of winning, especially if your opponent is a human, and not a computer.

The key move in this game is White's 21st. On this move I spent a recorded 31 minutes, perhaps the longest thinking time I have ever used on one move (I know many masters who take longer than this on one move in most of their 2-hour games, but doing so is not generally my style). On this 21st move I had to choose between the objectively correct move, which would retain a small advantage but almost force a draw, and a riskier, objectively poorer move which could leave me with a slight disadvantage, but gave my opponent a much greater chance of going astray.

I finally chose the riskier variation and was rewarded with almost instant victory. I don't remember getting a similar opportunity since then, but if similar conditions arise, the next time I won't hesitate 30 minutes before putting my opponent to the test.

Dan Heisman (2060) – Steve Schonhaut (1900)
Central Pennsylvania Open, Harrisburg 1970
Sicilian Defense

1.e4	c5
2.♘c3	d6
3.f4	...

The characteristic move of the Larsen Sicilian. I gave up this variation a few months later after being beaten by a couple of masters at the Pan-American Intercollegiate championships at Northwestern University.

3...	♘c6
4.♘f3	e6

5.♗b5	**♗d7**
6.O-O	**♘ge7**
7.♔h1 (5)	**a6**
8.♗xc6	**...**

Another move, 8.♗e2, is probably playable, but not very thematic. If I had played 7.♖e1, then 8.♗f1 would come under more serious consideration, although the idea of 8.♗f1 is more normal if White had played ♗g5 lines without f2-f4.

8...	**♘xc6**
9.d3 (9)	**g6**

This did not seem correct next to the "normal" 9...♗e7. 9...g6 violates the convention that, without a knight on e7, Black should not play both ...e6 and ...g6 in these types of positions.

10.f5 (15)   **...**

The first key move of the game. Opening up the position for the black bishops does not seem to follow the "rule" of keeping the position closed when your opponent has the two bishops. But the position trended more toward another "rule" to open up the game if you are better developed. Today I tend to play openings that lead much less frequently to this type of immediate confrontation – I wish to give my opponent more time to go wrong. Nevertheless, this pawn sacrifice cannot be completely condemned.

10...	**exf5**
11.exf5 (18)	**♗xf5**
12.♖e1+ (19)	**♗e7**

On 12...♗e6 13.d4! cxd4 14.♘xd4 ♘xd4 15.♕xd4 ♖g8 16.♘e4 ♗e7 17.♗f4, White gets good pressure.

13.♗h6 (22)   **♗e6**

Black defends against the threats of ♗g7-f6 and ♘d5.

14.d4 (30)	**cxd4**
15.♗g7?!	**...**

I do not know why I thought this was superior to 15.♘xd4. If then 15...♘xd4 16.♕xd4 ♗f6 17.♕d2 it seems that things are unclear, but certainly no worse for White than in the game.

[*R:* 15.♗g7 is weak. The only move to retain a White advantage is 15.♘xd4.]

15...   **♖g8**

16.♗xd4   **♘xd4**

[*R:* After 16...♕a5! Black is nicely better.]

17.♘xd4   **♕d7**

18.♕e2   **...**

White's advantage lies in his pressure on the e-file, superior development, lines for his pieces, and safer king. Black has the bishop pair and extra pawn, so threats of simplification are greatly in his favor. The net is perhaps a small advantage to White.

Position after 18.♕e2

18...   **♗f6!**

Correctly assessing his advantages, Black offers back the pawn for an easy endgame.

[*R:* At 17 ply, 18...♗f6 is not one of Black's seven best moves. Best is 18...♖f8 with a slight advantage to Black.]

19.♘xe6 (44)   **fxe6**

Of course not 19...♗xc3?? when 20.♘c5+ wins the queen.

20.♘d5 (45)

If 20.♕xe6+ ♕xe6 21.♖xe6+ ♔f7 22.♖xd6, then Black can simply play 22...♗xc3 23.bxc3 ♖fc8 24.♖d7+ ♔f6 25.♖xb7 ♖xc3 when Black has a pretty easy draw. As the higher-rated player, I wanted more.

20...   **♗d8**

This defends against the threat of ♘d5-b6.

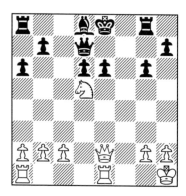

Position after 20...♗d8

It seems obvious that, compared to the line given after White's 20th move, taking the e-pawn should give White a better game than before, and it does – somewhat. However, after the "obvious" 21.♕xe6+ ♕xe6 22.♖xe6+ ♔d7, the fact that the king does not have to go to f7, as he did in the previous analysis to protect the bishop, is greatly in Black's favor as he can protect the d-pawn. After 23.♖1e1, 23...♖c8! with the dual defenses of both ...♖xc2 and ...♖c5 nullifies almost completely the better placement of White's pieces. So how can White play for a win?

If White tried the queen sortie, 21.♕c4, then I saw immediately that my problem was not the superficial 21...♖c8? 22.♖xe6+ ♕xe6 23.♘c7+ which not only wins the queen, but Black has no good moves, as 23...♗xc7 24.♕xe6+ attacks both rooks and 23...♖xc7 24.♕xe6+ forces 24...♔f8 when 25.♕xd6+ or 26.♖f1+ are both easy wins. If Black tries 22...♔f7, then 23.♖f1+ is still strong.

But my opponent was not rated much lower than I, and it seemed to me that with a little thought, he couldn't help but realize that I wouldn't be spending all this time refraining from winning the e-pawn just to set this silly trap (actually I spent much of my time seeing if I couldn't improve on the line starting with 21.♕xe6+). He would, after 21.♕c4, therefore look at any obvious moves carefully and would easily avoid ...♖c8, choosing among the three other defenses to the threat 22.♖xe6: 21...e5, 21...♔f7, and 21...♔f8.

Therefore I spent some time comparing 21.♕xe6+ with what might happen in these lines. My reasoning was, "Since I cannot win with 21.♕e6+, can I lose with 21.♕c4 ?" It turns out that maybe I run a little more chance of losing with 21.♕c4 than with 21.♕e6+, but in practice my chances of winning are greatly increased, so I played...

21.♕c4?!! (79)   ...

Now my opponent thought for a while and realized that 21...♖c8 was bad and decided he had to move his king. What he didn't know was that it made a big difference where he moved it, and he chose the wrong square!

21...   ♔f8?

The losing move! When I first annotated this game, I thought that this move didn't lose and that both 21...e5 and 21...♔f7 were better. As it turns out, 21...e5? also loses to the simple 22.♘f6+ when the forked queen and undefended rook on g8 cannot both be saved. Probably my opponent saw this variation as an extension to my 21...♖c8 "trap," but I didn't see 22.♘f6+ either during the game (since the line was never played, I didn't look very hard) or even when I first annotated it!

But 21...♔f7! is the game saver.

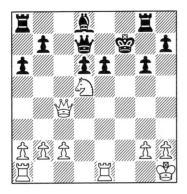

Position after 21...♔f7 (analysis)

Zarkov's computer analysis confirms, as I originally thought, that if Black plays carefully he gets a small advantage: 22.♕g4 ♖e8 23.♖e2 ♖c8 (23...h5? 24.♖f1+ ♔g7, when either 25.♕e4 { △ ♘f4,×g6}or 25.♕h3 both give White some winning chances.) 24.♖f1+ ♔g8 (again, if 24...♔g7 25.♘f4 ±) when White cannot simultaneously take advantage of both the e- and f- files, e.g. 25.♖fe1 ♕f7 (25...♔f7 =) 26.♖xe6 ♖xe6 27.♕xe6 ♕xe6 28.♖xe6 ♖xc2 29.♔g1 (or make *Luft* by advancing a pawn) 29...♗g5, and Black has winning chances. If after 25...♕f7 White instead tries 26.c4?, then 26...♗a5! is very good for Black. White can try 26.c3, but then Black is still somewhat better.

Was this possible disadvantage after 21...♔f7! worth the risk of playing 21.♕c4 ? I guess I certainly thought so. Since in the 21...♔f7 lines above *White* has to be careful not to lose, I was risking something by playing 21.♕c4.

[*R:* 21.♖ad1 seems best, with White retaining good chances, e.g. 21... e5 22.c4 ♖c7 23.b4 with initiative for White. After 21.♕c4 ♔f7 the game is fairly even.]

22.♘f4 +– (82)   **...**

This attack on e6 wins.

22...   **♔g7**

As mentioned earlier, I first thought Black could defend this position and that *this* was the losing move. I thought 22...e5 would hold. But then White wins with 23.♘e6+ because when the king moves to the e-file White can take advantage of the undefended rook, e.g., 23... ♔e7 24.♘c5! ♕e8 25.♕e6+ ♔f8 26.♕xd6+ ♔g7 (26...♕e7 27.♘e6+ ♔f7 28.♕xe5) 27.♖xe5 +– .

23.♘xe6+ (86)   **♔h6**

If worst comes to worst, White can simply meet other moves with 24.♘c7(+) winning a rook.

24.♖e3	**g5**
25.♖h3+	**1-0**

Just when the fun was beginning! My opponent, not a bad player, saw that there was no way I could not win! Rather than show you a bunch of analysis (most of it is easy), let me say that *Zarkov* looked at this position and announced mate in 7: 25...♔g6 26.♕e4+ ♔f7 27.♖xh7+ ♔e8 28.♘c7+ ♔f8 29.♖f1+ and mate after a couple of interpositions.

Game 22

We Win the U.S. Team Championship

In 1972, shortly after I graduated from Penn State, the old gang got together to form a team for the U.S. Team Championship. Especially appealing was that this was the only occasion Coach Donald Byrne agreed to play with us. Coach Byrne, once one of the three best players in the U.S. (shortly before Fischer rose to the top), played first board; I played second, Steve Wexler played third, Bill Bickham fourth, and Jim Joachim was the reserve.

In 1972 there were no regional U.S. Team Championships, so this tournament's winning team was the national champion. Two of our main rivals were teams from my native club, the Germantown Chess Club, with Richard Pariseau, Frank Camaratta, and Lou Golder, and a younger team from Temple University. The tournament was decided by a final-round game between Donald Byrne and Richard Pariseau. Rich only needed to draw to win the championship and could force a three-fold repetition. The only problem was that Rich was winning and Byrne was in his usual severe time trouble so, consistent with his aggressive temperament, Rich didn't want the draw! But then Rich made a blunder trying to win and Byrne was able to pull out a hair-raising win for the Championship.

In an earlier match we had been tied 1-1 with Temple after a Byrne win and a loss on fourth board. Steve had a bad position on third board, so I had no choice but to play on trying to win against Steve's former high school teammate, Eric Tobias, now a fellow member of the Chaturanga Chess Club. Up until move 43 I had been at best equal and normally would have been happy to get a draw, but after White blundered I immediately had to change my frame of mind and try to play for a win. A draw just wasn't good enough. While this game isn't up to the quality of the other games (after I achieved expert) in this book, it certainly shows my fighting spirit at a crucial time!

Eric Tobias (1950) – Dan Heisman (2060)
U.S. Team Championship, Philadelphia 1972
Temple vs. Penn State (Board 2)
Sicilian Defense
(50 moves in 2 hours)

1.e4	**c5**
2.♘f3	**d6**
3. d4	**cxd4**
4.♘xd4	**♘f6**
5.♘c3	**a6**

Still in my Najdorf "salad days."

6.♗c4	**e6**
7.♗b3	**♗e7**
8.f4	**b5** (1)

Sixteen years later, in *The Najdorf for the Tournament Player*, GM John Nunn states of 8...b5, "Universally condemned as bad, but matters are not so clear," and he quotes a game of his from 1980 which continued 9.e5 dxe5 10.fxe5 ♘fd7 11.♗xe6 ♘xe5 12.♗xc8 ♕xc8 13.♗f4 ♘bc6 14.♘xc6 ♘xc6 15.O-O O-O "with just a slight edge to White."

[*R:* Dr. Nunn's line is reasonable! White might try to improve with 14.♘d5 but even then his edge is minimal.]

9.a3 ...

On the other hand, this passive move gives Black few opening problems.

9...	**♗b7** (4.5)
10.♕f3	...

[*R:* Over the next several moves Black gradually outplays White. Here 10.O-O was slightly better but already White has missed his chance with 9.e5!.]

10... **O-O** (6.5)

10...♘bd7 first would discourage an eventual f4-f5, but gives White the opportunity to immediately sacrifice a piece at e6.

11.f5	**e5** (7.5)
12.♘de2	**♘bd7** (8)
13.♘g3	...

With this move White again plays passively and gives up the idea of g4-g5 in the near future.

13...   ♖c8 (11)

Around this time there were some nice grandmaster games where Black sacrificed the exchange on c3 to win the e-pawn.

14.♗e3   ♘b6 (16)

This is somewhat more aggressive than 14...♘c5.

15.0-0   ♘c4 (18)

An immediate 15...d5 was questionable as White takes and once Black takes with a knight White has the possibility of a pin with a rook on d1; while Black may escape by discovering an attack on White's queen via the bishop on b7, that was not the kind of quick skirmish I looked for against lower-rated players.

16.♗xc4   ♖xc4
17.♖ad1   ♕a8?! (21)

This idea doesn't work so well. Black should play ...h7-h6 first, or perhaps try another idea altogether.

[*R:* Misleading annotation. 17...♕a8 is best with a significant advantage to Black.]

18.♗g5! ±   ...

White puts his finger on Black's weak spot. With the bishop on e7 undefended, White can eliminate the knight on f6 which is defending d5, thus winning the strategic battle in the center.

[*Rybka* points out that 18.♗g5? is a tactical mistake which allows 18...♘xe4! 19.♘gxe4 ♗xg5 −+. If instead 19.♗xe7, then 19...♘xc3 wins easily.]

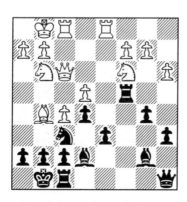

Position after 18.♗g5!

18...   ♖d8 (34)

Three minutes to blunder and 13 minutes to try to find a solution. I have often quoted the person who said, "The difference between a master and an expert is that a master thinks *before* he gets into trouble; an expert thinks *after* he gets into trouble." Here I play like the "expert" I am and think after I get into trouble!

19.♗xf6   ♗xf6 (35)
20.♕g4   ...

...And winning the kingside battle as well. Threats of 21.♘h5 △ Nf6+ are in the air.

20...   ♕a7+ (44)

Black swings the queen around to blunt the kingside attack.

21.♔h1   ♕e3 (44)

[*R:* 21...d5! is a shot due to the pin on the fourth rank.]

22.♖d3   ♕g5 (49)
23.♕xg5   ♗xg5 (49)

I have blunted the attack on the kingside, but White has everything to gain and little to lose in this type of position. My only hope is that later my two bishops will find a position where they can do some dirty work.

24.♖1d1   ♗e7 (51)
25.♔g1   ♔f8 (59)
26.♔f2   h6 (68.5)

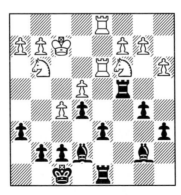

Position after 26...h6

At this point I put "△" on my scoresheet, an indication to myself to look at the game later and see if I can find a good plan at the marked point. That explains the 9 minutes I used.

27.♔f3	**g6 (74)**
28.fxg6	**...**

This is not necessary, as Black can't easily take on f5, but it really doesn't hurt White all that much either. He still has an advantage.

28...	**fxg6 (74)**
29.♘f1	**♔f7 (81)**

[According to *Rybka*, 29...♔g7 is better. After 29...♔f7 the game is even.]

30.♘e3	**♖4c8 (82)**
31.♘ed5	**♗xd5**
32.♖xd5	**♔e6 (83)**
33.♖5d3	**...**

And so White continues to sit on a nice advantage. Notice how much better his knight is than Black's bishop.

[*Rybka* still rates the game about even.]

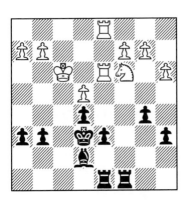

Position after 33.♖5d3

33...	**♖f8+**
34.♔e2	**♖f7 (84)**
35.♖f1	**♖xf1**

Getting rid of a pair of rooks slightly eases Black's defensive task – but by this point I realized I'd probably have to try to win!

36. ♔xf1   **♖c4** (91)

[*R:* A mistake! Black should have played 36...♗g5 ∓.]

37.♔e2   **♗g5** (92)

Without the extra pair of rooks, I can keep my rook on c4 and still activate my bishop – a little. I actually have my first threat in what seems like the whole game, 38...♗c1, hence...

38.♔d1   **b4** (95)

Again, every little bit of opening on the board gives my rook and bishop a little more scope and targets for attack. Just defending against White's center control would be hopelessly passive. The position now is close to equal.

39.axb4   **♖xb4** (95)
40.b3   **♗f4** (97)

Seeing if I can either get him to put his pawns on dark squares (41. g3) or give my bishop some dark squares to invade (41.h3).

41.h3   **...**

White has all his pawns on white squares – no targets for my bishop.

41...   **♗g5(!)**

Black is trying to put White in a mild *Zugzwang*. If the king moves, Black gets in ...♗g5-c1 △ ...♗b2 with some activation of the bishop. If the knight moves, the e-pawn falls immediately. White can move the rook and allow ...♖b4-d4+, but after 42.♖g3 ♖d4+ 43.♖d3 (other moves lose material) Black can try 43...♗e3!? or just 43...♖xd3 44.cxd3 ♗e3 when Black has activated his bishop. Whether the king or rook moves, the position is still very equal.

42.♔e2   **♗c1** (103)

[*R:* Better was 42...a5 ±. Now White gets a big advantage with 43.♔f3, but...]

Again I put the " △ " on my scoresheet – two in one game is close to a record for me! Searching for a plan (and double-checking my tactics on a superficial "trap") is why I used 6 of my remaining 23 minutes on this move; now I am down to 8 moves in 17 minutes – plenty for most, but I like to leave some room to avoid error.

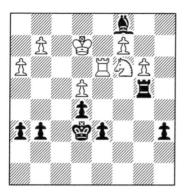

Position after 42...♗c1

43.♘a2??   ...

White makes a move unworthy of his rating. While a weaker player might be enticed by this fork, a player of Eric's caliber missing the fact that 43.♘a2 loses material can only be explained as an oversight. I don't have Eric's time recorded, but since there were only a few moves to go before time control this looks like a classic time-trouble blunder. The position shifts from "White is better but almost undoubtedly not winning," to "Black is better and close to winning."

43...   **♖xe4+**

With check. And now if White attacks the rook with 44.♔f3, Black saves everything after 44...♖f4+.

44.♔d1   ...

And now, with Board 3 losing, I must play for a win!

44...   **♗g5** (104)
45.c4   **♖f4** (110.5)

I use almost half my time looking for a plan to infiltrate.

[*Rybka* says 45...♖e3 is better and retains winning chances.]

46.♔e2   **♖f7**
47.♖d1   ...

[*R:* 47.♘b4 ♖a7 48.♘d5 reduces Black's winning chances.]

47...   **♗h4**
48.♖f1   **♖b7** (116)

I would rather delay a decision such as whether it is good to trade rooks until I have some more time to think how I might win; at this point I just want to make time control and preserve my advantage.

49.♖f3   **♗f6** (118)
50.♖g3   **♔f5**

Time control. I am much better, but am I winning? The pressure is surely on White now, who must draw to win the match.

[*R:* 51...a5 should be winning.]

51.♖f3+   **...**

You can almost always count on a player who is losing to repeat moves, even though sometimes it is bad for him. For example, sometimes you spot a move you missed and by repeating your opponent gives you the chance to improve. Psychologically, it is hard for him to avoid "asking for the draw."

51...   **♔e6** (121)
52.♖g3   **g5** (121)

Black blocks in his bishop, but of course he doesn't want a draw! [*R:* Again, 52...a5 is best.]

53.♖e3   **d5** (124)

At last! The classic Sicilian break move. I never thought I'd get it in (I'm being sarcastic). [*Rybka:* Better is waiting with 53...a5 or 53...♗d8.]

54.cxd5   **♔xd5** (124.5)

I have a passed pawn, but White can easily blockade the light squares in front of it. I need more to win.

55.♖d3+   **♔e6** (126)
56.♔f3   **...**

Trying to cause problems on all the kingside light squares.

56...   **♗e7** (128)
57.♔e4   **♖b6** (130.5)

The reduced material makes it difficult for Black to make progress.

58.g4   **♗c5** (132)

[In *Rybka's* judgment, 58...♗c5? is a mistake, allowing 59.♖d5 with good drawing chances for White. After 59...♗d4 60.♖xb5 axb5 White should be able to blockade the light squares.]

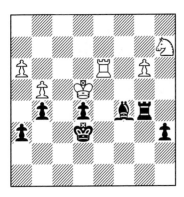

Position after 58...♗c5

59.♘c1?? ...

Looks like my opponent should leave his knight alone! The knight, which had remained motionless on the seemingly useless a2 square since the fatal fork on move 43, now moves again and ruins the defense! In this particular position, White would have to move his rook before attempting to move the knight. With White tied up this way, Black still has some winning tries, such as penetrating on the a-file. For example, if Black had his rook on a5, he might be able to get behind White's pieces. White has to play carefully to defend; for example, if we place the black rook on a5 with all the other pieces the same, then if White tries 1.b4?, the reply 1...♗xb4 2.♘xb4 ♖a4 3.♖b3 a5 would win for Black. But after 59.♘c1?? it is all over.

59... **♖b4+ (133)**

Winning the rook after 60.♔f3 e4+, so...

0-1

Game 23

I Win the Philadelphia Invitational Championship

In the late 1960's, Rich Pariseau "invented" the Philadelphia Closed Championship. The best eight players in Philadelphia were invited for a two-weekend round robin. This tournament was dominated in the first five years by Pariseau, Dr. Leroy Dubeck, Mike Shahade, and Ross Nickel, among others. I was an eager spectator and when my rating finally became high enough to be invited, Rich informed me that he wasn't inviting me – he didn't want to disturb my studies at Penn State! I was greatly disappointed, especially since I was to graduate as the valedictorian and felt that the decision should be mine, not Rich's. Very uncharacteristically, I vowed to Rich that after I graduated I would play in the Philadelphia Championship and win it!! Rich gave me that unbelieving look of his and intimated that if I did as I promised he would be impressed.

A year after I graduated I did get a chance to play in my first Philadelphia Championship. By then the "old guard" was being replaced by a stronger, young new group: Bruce Rind, Tim Taylor, Boris Baczynskyj, Karl Dehmelt, and the Costigan brothers. Shahade would join this group to form the Philadelphia team in the U.S. Phone League in the mid-'70s. By 1973 Taylor and Baczynskyj were in the Philadelphia Championship, joined by bright young star Mike Pastor, who would play in the U.S. Junior Invitational the year that it was held in Philadelphia, won by some young guy named Larry Christiansen, now a strong GM.

To make a long story short, I did win the Philadelphia Invitational with my most impressive performance to date, 5.5-1.5. However, Pariseau was not very impressed! He noted that since the old guard – most of the past competitors – hadn't played, the level of competition was not as tough. In retrospect, it was probably tougher, but the Taylors, Baczynskyjs, and Pastors didn't quite yet have a name for themselves as did the old guard, even though their ratings were already surpassing their predecessors'.

Winning the title brought my rating up to about 2227, using the rating algorithm then in effect. However, in a move that was to strongly affect my entire chess career, the U.S. Chess Federation took this title away from me *ex-post facto* with a strange decision at the 1973 U.S. Open (held in August) to change the rating system, *affecting games previously played but not yet rated*(!), thus costing me about 40 rating points from my estimated rating from my Philadelphia Closed Invitational victory, played in July.

Since full computerization was not yet in use to calculate ratings, games from a month or more earlier were not yet rated and affected. Thus players like myself, who had gained points to achieve a master title within the previous month, could likely find themselves without the title, even though the rating rules in force *at the time the games were played* would make one a master. It is important to note that, at the time, master was a much more difficult title to achieve than it was to be in later years. This was grossly unfair, as USCF should have only put the rating change into effect for games played after the change was announced.

This strange USCF decision permanently altered my perception of USCF from benevolent (as perceived by me via Colonel Edmondson) to somewhat untrustworthy and chaotic. It also made me quit chess for a while, as I perceived I was being treated quite unfairly. *Ex-post facto* decisions will do that to you! Since then I have never played as frequently as I once did, even though by 1973 I had already been curtailing my playing time somewhat.

Enough history. Here is my game against Pastor.

Mike Pastor (~2200) – Dan Heisman (2100)
Philadelphia Invitational Championship 1973
King's *Indian Attack*
(40 moves in 2 hours)

1.♘f3	d6 (2)
2.g3	c5 (2.5)
3.♗g2	♘c6 (3)
4.0-0	g6 (3)
5.e4	♗g7 (3)
6.d3	e6 (5)

Mike out-finesses me in this opening. The system with e6 is much better against the Closed Sicilian, where White has already committed to ♘b1-c3 and can't easily play c3-d4 as Mike does with advantage. Black should try a system with ...♘f6/0-0 or with ...e7-e5. For example, 6...♘f6 7.♘c3 0-0 leads to a position where Fischer, possibly somewhat tongue-in-cheek, says Black may be somewhat better. Of course, White could still renounce ♘c3 for c2-c3 and d3-d4 in these lines, too by playing first ♘bd2, which is probably correct and preserves White's small advantage.

7.c3	**♘ge7** (6)
8.d4	**O-O** (8.5)

White has gotten a clear advantage out of the opening.

9.♗g5	**h6** (12)
10.♗e3	**cxd4** (16)

Lacking a plan, Black cedes the center. But if 10...♕b6, then 11.b4!.

11.cxd4	**♗d7** (17)

[*Rybka* assesses 11...d5 as better and at least equalizing, e.g. 12.e5 ♘f5.]

12.♕d2	**♔h7** (17)
13.♘c3	**♖c8** (19.5)
14.h4?!	**d5** (22.5)

Now that White has committed himself on the kingside, Black looks to figure out what to do in the center.

15.e5	**♘f5** (24)
16.♗f4!?	**♕e7** (26)
17.♖fd1	**♕b4** (28.5)
18.g4	**...**

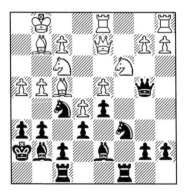

Position after 18.g4

Mike tactically guards the d-pawn from harm. While it looks like Black might take advantage of the hanging bishop on f4, the line 18...♘fxd4?! doesn't work because of 19.♘xd4 ♘xd4 20.a3!, and not 20.♕xd4?! ♖c4 when Black might justify the tactics.

18...	♞**fe7** (29)
19.♖ac1	♞**a5(?)** (38.5)

When first annotating this game I thought 19...b5!? here might provide the right queenside play and it is better than the move I chose. However, in analyzing this game on the computer it insisted during this part of the game on playing 19...f6, taking advantage of the fact that the g-pawn has advanced and the bishop and knight on the f-file can become targets for the rook on f8.

[*R:* 19...♞a5 may be best! But White retains a slight advantage on any reasonable move by Black.]

20.b3	♛**b6** (43)
21.♗f1 ±	...

White continues to hold his small but distinct opening advantage.

21...	♖**c7** (46)
22.♗d3	...

Now the plans with ...f7-f6 aren't quite so appealing, as g6 becomes a target.

22...	♖**8c8** (47.5)
23.♞e2	♖**xc1** (49.5)
24.♖xc1	♖**xc1+**
25.♞xc1	♞**5c6** (54)

25...♞7c6, pushing queenside play, was also possible, but Black might quickly find all his pieces "offsides" if White starts throwing pieces at the kingside.

26.h5	♛**a5** (56)
27.hxg6+	...

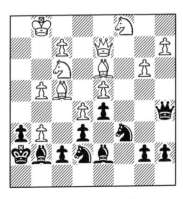

Position after 27.hxg6+

Without black rooks to penetrate the f-file, White logically initiates the pressure on g6.

27...	**fxg6** (56.5)
28.♕c2	**♕b6** (61)

Here the idea of 28...♘b4? is dubious, since White has 29.♗d2! ♘xc2?? 30.♗xa5 ♘a3 31.♗b4.

29.♕c3	**♕a5** (64.5)
30.♕b2	**♗e8** (66.5)

But now the computer said that 30...♘b4 is worth trying here, as the trick 31.♗d2? doesn't work.

31.♗d2	**♕b6?** (68.5)

White's careful maneuvering pays off as Black blunders and allows additional positional pressure. Both 31...♕c7 and 31...♕d8 were much better.

[*R:* Wrong again. 31...♕b6 is best! But still White retains that painfully persistent small advantage. This position is no fun to play as Black! But my patience eventually pays off...]

32.b4   ...

Now I realize I have new problems and need a new plan. White threatens to bring the knight from c1 to b3 to c5 and my queen is blocking the preventive move ...b7-b6.

32...   **♕c7** (81.5)

I could also consider 32...♘a5!?, when a likely continuation would be 33.♕c2 ♘c4. I have to sacrifice this pawn to open up lines for my pieces, but my light-squared bishop will be strong. 34.♗xc4 dxc4 35.♕xc4 ♗c6 36.♘h4 ♗d5 and Black has some compensation for his pawn minus.

[*R:* Yes, this time you are correct. 32...♘a5 is much better.]

33.♘b3   ...

33.b5!? is a consideration. [*R:* Prefer slightly 33.♘e2 ± or 33.♕c3 ±.]

33...	**♘d8** (84.5)
34.b5	**♘c8?!** (89)

[According to *Rybka*, Black is getting dangerously close to losing. Better was 34...b6.]

35.♘c5   ...

White could also play 35.♘h4 △ ♕b1, a2-a4 ± (×g6) [*R:* Yes, 35.♘h4 is likely winning.]

35...   **♘b6!?** (95)

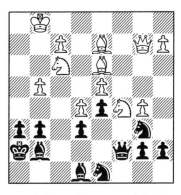

Position after 35...♘b6!?

Black is starting to inject some life into his defense. The more "normal" ...b7-b6 is also possible.

36.a4?   **...**

Black's active defense starts to pay off! White should have continued cautiously with 36.♕c2 △ g4-g5, ♘h4 ±. If instead 36.♗a5, then Black has the reply 36...♕f7.

[According to the chess engine, this is another bad evaluation. 36.a4! is best.]

36...   **♘c4** (97)
37.♗xc4   **...**

Another possibility was 37.♕c2 ♘xd2 △...b7-b6, ...♕c7-f7 when White's advantage would hinge on his being able to blunt Black's queen with f2-f4.

37...   **dxc4**

The situation has changed. The pressure on g6 is lessened and for his weak e- and c-pawns Black has much more active possibilities.

38.♗b4   **...**

[*R:* 38.♘e4! was the appropriate consideration and White has excellent winning chances.]

38...   **a6(?)** (100)

Although this is a logical follow-up to ...♘c4 (both are part of a plan to activate Black's light-squared bishop) this move is dangerous at this particular time. I wanted to break up the queenside pawn structure, where White has the spatial advantage, but I give White some return tactical shots. Just 38...♕f7 seems called for.

[*R:* Wrong, wrong, wrong again! The move played, 38...a6!, was the correct way to refute White's last move. *Sometimes a player sees or feels more about what is going on during a game than he does under cool consideration afterwards!*]

39.bxa6　　　　bxa6(?) (100)

I played this "obvious" recapture instantly, but there were alternatives such as ...♗c6 or ...b7-b6 △ ...♗xa4.

[39...bxa6 is fine, says *Rybka*. White only has a slight advantage.]

40.♕c3　　　　...

Of course not 40.♘xa6?? ♕b7–+ [*R:* But 40.♕e2 is more accurate. After 40.♕c3 ♗c6, White has only a small advantage.]

40...　　　　♕f7 (103.5)

When I first annotated this game, I thought this was a very good move that equalized. Upon further inspection it is possibly the best move, but not as special as I thought, and it soon leads to a dangerous position.

41.♘h2?!　　　　...

[*R:* 41.♘h2! is best.]

41...　　　　♕f4? (107)

Although this looks superficially appealing, this first move after time control is weak.

[*R:* Yup! Better are 41...♘b7 or 41...a5.]

42.♘xa6?　　　　...

White misses his last great chance to get back his big advantage. After 42.♗a5! he will remove the defender of the e6-pawn and make Black solve some very difficult defensive problems. In that case a possible line would run: 42.♗a5 ♘c6 43.♘xe6 ♕e4, and either:

A) 44.♕e1!? ♕xe1 45.♗xe1 ♘xd4!? 46.♘xd4 ♗xe5 △ ...♗xa4, or

B) 44.f3 ♕b1+ 45.♘f1 ♕d1! 46.♗b6 ♕xa4 47.♘xg7 ♔xg7
(computer analysis at the end of this game thanks to *Zarkov*)

[*R:* 42.♗a3 is best, when after 42...♗f8 43.♗c1 ♕f7 44.♘e4 White still has a nice advantage.]

Instead he removes the attacker of the e6 square and the game starts to turn around. Notice that Black's light-squared bishop is starting to exert power, a direct consequence of the active 35...♞b6.

42...   ♝xa4 (108)
43.♞c5   ...

[*R:* 43.♛e3 keeps Black's advantage to a minimum, but likely Mike was still dreaming of winning!]

43...   ♝c6 (111)
44.♝a3   ...

Again, at first annotation, I thought that 44.♝a5!? was still good, but Black has 44...♞b7!! 45.♞xe6 (45.♞xb7 ♝xb7 46.♛xc4 ♝xe5 –+) 45...♛e4 46.f3 ♛d5! 47.♞xg7 ♞xa5 48.♞e6 ♞b3 ∓.

[*R:* 44.♛e3 or 44.♛d2 would minimize the damage.]

44...   ♝d5 (117)

Making room for the knight at c6. For the first time in the game, Black now has the advantage and initiative.

45.♝c1   ...

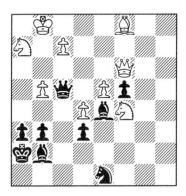

Position after 45.♝c1

45...   ♛f7! (121)

A draw would be a big boost to my morale here, so I offered one at this point. Mike, of course, was the up-and-coming superstar and I was just an out-of-hibernation non-contender. Mike therefore declined and I began perhaps my most memorable queen maneuver.

[*R:* Yup, correct and memorable!]

46.f4?!   ...

While 46.f3 is safer, 46.f4 does allow White some tactical shots later that would have given him a chance to save the game. That is why I have refrained from saying that Black is winning by force here.

46... ♛a7! (127)

47.♘f1 ...

On 47.♛b2, Black has moves like 47...♝f8 and ...♘c6 to continue to cause problems on the queenside. After either 47.♘f1 or the safer 47.♛b2 Black is somewhat better.

47... ♛a2! (129)

[*R:* here 47...♝f8 was the best way for Black to maintain a nice advantage.]

48.♘e3? ...

But now White brings himself to the edge of the precipice. He had to cut off the second rank with 48.♘d2 or 48.♛b2, when Black retains an edge, but is not really close to winning.

[*R:* Wrong again. 48.♘e3 is best, or at least close to best.]

48... ♛e2! (130)

Originally I thought this definitely won by force, but *Zarkov* found one last resource for White to save the game.

49.♛d2? ...

But this isn't it! White must play 49.f5! when the hanging d5 bishop gives White the defense 49...♛f3 50.f6 ♝f8, and White still has some good chances.

49... ♛f3 (132)

Finishing the queen tour, which started one square away on f4!!

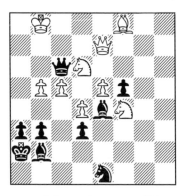

Position after 49...♛f3

50.♕h2?   ...

White might have been losing, but this makes it easy for Black. Mike is clearly discouraged by the turn of events and misses his only continuation 50.f5!. Now that Black is guarding his d5-bishop this gives up a pawn on f5, but eliminates Black's immediate attack. White would still have excellent practical chances to save the game. Instead Black just overwhelms White's position with...

50...   ♘c6 (134)

51.♕b2   ...

There are too many threats and nothing matters any more. If 51.g5 then 51...♘xd4 52.gxh6? ♘e2+. [If I remember correctly, Mike, who had been very enthusiastic before the game and confident throughout, now began to realize the hopelessness of his situation. I know the feeling!]

51...   ♕g3+

52.♘g2   ...

52.♔f1 ♕xf4+.

52...   ♘xd4 (144)

The white queen cannot simultaneously guard d4 and g2, so not only does a pawn fall, but another dangerous attacker enters the area.

53.♗e3   c3 (149)

This is so cute that at first I thought it deserved an exclamation point for advancing with tempo, taking advantage of the overworked queen. However, Black could also win with 53...♘f3+ 54.♔f1 ♘h2+ 55.♔g1 (trying to hold onto material) 55...♗xg2! because if 56.♕xg2 ♘f3+.

54.♕f2   ♘f3+ (149)

55.♔f1   ♗c4+

Not only did 53...c3 deflect the queen, it opened up this line for the bishop.

56.♘d3   ...

Obviously, Mike could have resigned here or on the previous move, but I think he was in shock and hoping for a miracle.

56...   ♗xd3+

0-1

No moves, no miracles. This game put me on my way with a second straight victory, this one over one of the pre-tournament favorites.

Game 24:

On the Road to Master (Again)

This is one of my all-time favorite games and it contains one of my all-time favorite moves. I hadn't played in quite a while, but Ken Potts, one of the area's affable young masters, kept telling me that with the rating inflation of the late 1970's, I could now become active without even studying and easily get a master's rating. Since the reader now knows that had been a sore spot with me, I was curious and took up the challenge. My first tournament back I won with an undefeated 4-0, beating Ross Nickel in a crucial game. This put me on the doorstep. Then, with an undefeated score of 6½-3½ at the strong 1981 Franklin-Mercantile Chess Club Masters-Experts Invitational, I finally achieved a published master title.

At the time my "second" title was achieved, there were fewer than twenty active masters in Pennsylvania and 500 in the U.S.

My opponent in my best game from this event is friend Richard Lunenfeld, a lawyer and fellow former member of the Germantown Chess Club, where I did much of my chess learning.

Dan Heisman (2140) – Richard Lunenfeld (2200)
Franklin-Mercantile Experts-Masters
Cherry Hill, New Jersey 1981
French Defense
(40 moves in 2 hours)

1.e4	e6
2.d4	d5
3.♘d2	♘c6

Rich always plays the French Defense, but not always this Guimard variation, which I happen to respect.

4.♘1f3	♘f6
5.e5	♘d7
6.c3?! (1)	...

Undoubtedly better is the recommended 6.♘b3.

6...   **f6**

7.♗b5!? (4)   **...**

I played the same rare move order against Rich in 1972 in New York. He remembered that opening. I didn't even remember that we had played that game!

7...   **a6?! (3)**

Perhaps Black should try 7...fxe5, forcing White to recapture with the pawn, for if 8.♘xe5? ♘cxe5 9.dxe5 c6 10.♗d3 ♘xe5 11.♕h5+ ♘f7 is good for Black.

8.♗xc6 (5)   **bxc6**

9.0-0 (5.5)   **fxe5(?)**

This eradicates most of White's opening concerns. Both 9...♗e7 and 9...c5 are better.

10.♘xe5 (8)   **♘xe5**

11.dxe5 (8)   **♕h4!? (28)**

This is an interesting sally which I anticipated. Its point is to dominate the kingside and simultaneously prevent White from dominating the kingside with *his* queen. The loss of tempo for Black here is insignificant. Other tries are 11...c5 or 11...♗e7 12.♕h5+ g6 13.♕f3 ♖f8 14.♕h3 ♖f7 =.

[*R:* 11...a5 is best, and if 12.♕g4 ♕d7 13.♖d1 h5, and White's advantage is only slightly more than a normal opening edge (about a quarter-pawn instead of a tenth). After 11...♕h4(?) White's advantage is much larger.]

12.♘f3 (15.5)   **♕g4 (45)**

13.h3 (17)   **...**

I want his queen off the fourth rank for my following maneuver.

13...   **♕h5 (48)**

14.♕a4!? (20)   **♗d7**

15.♕a5 (21)   **♔d8 (52)**

White has succeeded in preventing Black from castling, but what is he to do now? In retrospect, this position is better for White, but in practice it is much easier to play for Black, who has a clear plan: a quick and nasty kingside attack. How should White proceed to preserve his advantage?

[*R:* White's last few moves have been very accurate but this move is not. Better is 15...♖c8, but after 16.b3 White has a nice advantage.]

16.c4!! (38)   **...**

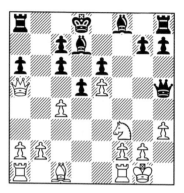

Position after 16.c4!!

A rather stunning move; one of the most subtle I have ever played. Superficially, the move looks weak: Any threat to take on d5, giving the d7-bishop life, especially with an attack on h3, seems just plain dumb. But other moves do not accomplish anything: 16.♗e3 h6 17.♗c5 g5 and Black has good attacking prospects. Of course, 16.♗g5+? ♔c8 17.c4 h6 only helps Black.

[Computers have a way of being spoilsports, especially with regards to what I formerly thought was one of my all-time best moves (I still like it!). *Rybka* likes 16.c4, but slightly prefers 16.♗g5+ ♔c8 17.♖ad1 h6 18.♗e3 g5 and then 19.c4 with a winning position.]

16...　　　　　　　　♗e7(?) (57)

It is understandable that Black does not yet sense the danger and, having used half his time, plays the natural developing and attacking move. It is difficult to prove, but this may be the losing move; 16...h6 or maybe 16...dxc4?! may save the game. [R: 16...♗e7 is as good as Black has in a bad position.]

For after...

17.cxd5! (41.5)　　　　　**...**

...Black begins to realize that White has a very strong attack. Now he uses most of his remaining time searching for a defense.

17...　　　　　　　　**exd5 (96)**

If 17...cxd5 18.♗e3 ♖f8 19.♖fc1 ♖c8 20.♖xc7! ♖xc7 21.♖c1 (with ♗e3-b6 in reserve) wins easily.

[R: The more I look at 17...cxd5!, the more I think Black might be able to save the game with it. After 18.♗d2 ♖f8 19.♖ac1 ♔e8 20.♗b4 ♗xb4

21.♕xb4 ♖xf3 22.gxf3 ♖c8 23.♖fe1 ♕xh3 24.♖e3, White retains winning chances but it is not easy.]

18.e6! (45)   ...

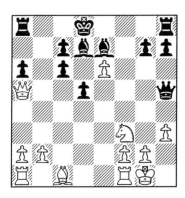

Position after 18.e6!

The point! As planned on move 16, White practices the theme of line clearance for his queen's bishop and rook – both on the h2-b8 diagonal and on the e-file! A rare practical theme. The target is Black's king. White's attack comes first and stronger.

18...   ♗xe6 (98)
19.♗f4 (46)   ♖c8 (100.5)

Of course not 19...♗d6?? 20.♗xd6. Nor would 19...♖a7? be of any help. The rook would be out of play and subject to lines forking it from c5 later (compare ...♖a7 to the game continuation).

20.♖fe1 (65)   ...

The "simple" 20.♘d4 is good, but not quite as good: 20...♗d7 (20...♗xh3 21.♘xc6+ ♚d7 22.♕a4) 21.♕xa6 ♕g6 22.♗g3 ± e.g., 22...h5 23.♘f3 ♗xh3? 24.♘e5!.

20...   ♗xh3!? (101)

Black correctly does not wish to sit passively by and let White attack him. While a move like 20...♗xh3 is difficult to prove as best, moves like this are often the best practical chance in these positions – they give your opponent a chance to go wrong, and make him worry a little about *your* threats.

21.♖xe7! (72)   ...

[*R:* Yes, this wins but 21.♗xc7+! ♖xc7 22.♖xe7 is better.]

21...   ♕g4?!

If Black accepts the rook, 21...♔xe7, 22.♕c5+ is the main line. I gave this position to *Zarkov*, let it think overnight, and it decided White was much better. However, when I went to break down the lines, there were so many subtleties and sub-variations that I decided it was better to just provide an overview of the main lines:

A) 22...♔f6 23.♕xc6+ ♔e7 24.♗g5+ ♔f8 25.♕c5+ ♔g8 26.gxh3:

Position after 26.gxh3 (analysis)

and now I had expected – and calculated – only 26...♕xh3? when 27.♕xc6! wins: 27...♕xf3?? 28.♕e6+. But Black does have a defense in this line: 26...h6! ⩲. I have analyzed this position with humans and with a computer, and come to the conclusion that White is at best microscopically better, but that is about it. Black's *Luft* allows him to survive White's attack, whether after 27.♘e5 or 27.♖e7. If anyone can find a winning line here, I sure would like to see it!

B) 22...♔f7 23.♘g5+ ♔g8 24.♕xc6 ♖d8 (24...♗g4 25.♕xd5+ ♔f8 26.f3+−) 25.♘xh3 ♕f7 26.♗xc7 ♖c8 27.♖c1.

C) 22...♔d7 23.♘e5+ ♔e6 24.gxh3, and:

C1) 24...♖hd8 25.♖e1 ♖e8 26.♕xc6+ ♔f5 27.♕xd5.

C2) 24...♖he8 25.♕xc6+ ♔f5 (25...♔e7 26.♕xd5 ♕f5 27.♖e1 ♔f8 28.♘d7+ +−) 26.♕xd5 ♖cd8 (26...♔xf4?? 27.♘d3#) 27.♘d7+ ♔g6 28.♕c6+ +−.

C3) 24...♔f5 25.♘xc6! ♔xf4 (25...♕xh3 26.♗xc7 ♖cf8 27.♕xd5+) 26.♕e3+ ♔f5 27.♕e5+ ♔g6 28.♘e7+ ♔h6 (28...♔f7 29. ♕xh5) 29.♘f5+ ♔g6 30.♕e6+ ♔g5 31.f4+.

C4) 24...♕xh3? 25.♕xc6+ ♔f5 26.♕d7+ wins the queen.

22.♖d7+?! (82)   **...**

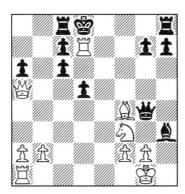

Position after 22.♖d7+?!

A move worthy of a diagram! Flashy and forcing but faulty. I do get some credit for trying to keep the game complicated when Rich has much less time. Three months after the game I found the best line: 22.♗xc7+! (which I had looked at, but rejected during the game) 22...♔xe7 23.♕c5+ ♔f6 (23...♔d7 24.♕d6+) 24.♕xc6+ ♕e6 25.♕c3+!. This is the move I had not seen during the game. At that time I analyzed 25...♔g6 26.gxh3, and now Black's awkward king placement immediately puts his game in jeopardy. For instance, 26...♖hf8 (26...d4 is actually better) 27.♖e1! and White's attack breaks through and wins immediately.

But it was not quite so simple. Years later, computer analysis showed that White had an improvement in the analysis above by playing the *Zwischenzug* 26.♖e1 (instead of 26.gxh3), when after 26...♕f6 27.♘e5+ ♔g5 White has an easy win with 28.♕g3+ ♔h5 29.♕xh3+ ♔g5 30.♘f3+ ♔g6 31.♕g4+ ♔f7 32.♘e5+.

However, *one move earlier* in the same line from the previous paragraph, Black had a tougher defense with the deflection 25...d4 (after 25.♕c3+, instead of 25...♔g6). This deflection, while still losing, provides Black two benefits: The black queen has escape routes along the a2-g8 diagonal, and in many lines Black avoids losing his bishop with check. White would have to play exactly (analysis aided by *Zarkov*): 26.♕xd4+ ♔g6 27.♖e1, when:

A) 27...♕xa2 28.♘e5+! when Black has:

A1) 28...♔f5 29.g4+ and

A1a) 29... ♔g5 30.♕e3+ is mate in four: 30...♔f6 31.♕f4+ ♔e7 32.♘c6+ ♔d7 33.♕d6#.

A1b) 29...♔f6 30.♕f4+ transposes to "A1a."

A1c) 29...♔e6 30.♕d6#.

A1d) 29...♗xg4 30.♕xg4+ ♔f6 31.♕f4+ and mate as in "A1a."

A2) 28...♔g5 29.g3! and

A2a) 29...♖hf8 30.♕h4+ mates: 30...♔f5 31.♕f4+ ♔e6 32.♘d7+ ♔xd7 (or 32...♔d5 33.♕e4#) 33.♕d6#.
A2b) 29...♔f6 30.♘c6+! ♔g6 31.♘e7+ ♔f7 32.♕f4+ ♔e8 33.♘d5+ ♗e6 34.♖xe6 ♔d7 35.♕d6#.

B) 27...♕f6 28.♘e5+, when either

B1) 28...♔h5 29.g4+ ♔h4 30.♘f3+! (see diagram):

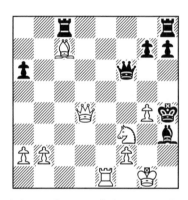

Position after 30.♘f3+! (analysis)

30...♕xf3 31.♗g3+ ♕xg3 (31...♔g5 32.♕xg7#) 32.fxg3+ +−.

B2) 28...♔h6 29.♕e3+ ♔h5 (29...♕g5 30.♘f7+) 30.♕xh3+ ♔g5 31.♘f3+ ♔g6 32.♖e6 wins the queen.

B3) 28...♔g5 29.♕e3+ ♔h5 (29...♕f4 30.♘f7+ and 31.♗xf4) 30.♕xh3+ transposes to "2."

So White is winning after 22.♗xc7+, but having missed this it is Black's turn to wend his way through the complications.

22...   **♔e8?? (117)**

Rich took almost all his remaining time to try to find the defense, so I can't really blame him for failing. However, Black does have a saving loophole. During the game I saw the best defense, 22...♕xd7□ 23.♗g5+ ♔e8 24.♖e1+, and I thought I was winning , but I failed to see that Black has two(!) saving lines:

A) 24...♔f8 25.♕c5+ (or 25.♕a3+) 25...♔g8 26.gxh3 and now I had expected – and calculated – only 26...♕xh3? when 27.♕xc6! wins: 27... ♕xf3?? 28.♖e6+. But Black does have a defense in this line: 26...h6! ±. I have analyzed this position with humans and with a computer, and come to the conclusion that White is at best microscopically better, but that is about it. Black's *Luft* allows him to survive White's attack, whether after 27.♘e5 or 27.♖e7. If anyone can find a winning line here, I sure would like to see it!

[R: If 22...♕xd7 23.♖e1! wins by force!].

B) 24...♗e6 25.♘d4 ♔f7 26.♖xe6 ♖he8 when Black holds:

B1) 27.♖xc6?! ♖e4 28.♕a4□ ♖e1+ (28...♖xd4?? 29.♖f6+ ♔e7 30.♖xa6+ ♔e8 31.♖e6+ wins the queen) 29.♔h2 ♕g4 30.f4 ♖e3 =.
B2) 27.♖xe8 ♖xe8 28.♗e3 ♕d6 29.♕xa6 c5 30.♕xd6 cxd6 31.♘b5 ♖e6! (31...♖d8? 32.♗f4! ±) 32.♘c7 (32.♗f4 allows 32...♖e1+ 33.♔h2 ♖e2 with counterplay) 32...♖e5 33.♔f1 ∞/=.

23.♕e1+ ...

Rich missed this nice retreating move, which I had foreseen. Because of the threat of mate, Black has no time to recapture his material, so the rest needs little comment.

23... ♕e6

Not 23...♔xd7 24.♘e5+ winning the queen.

24.♖xg7	♔f8
25.♕xe6	♗xe6
26.♗h6	♔e8 (119)
27.♖e1	1-0

175

Game 25

Playing Postal Chess With Computer Help

I once saw a comment in Alex Dunne's *Chess Life* column noting that his challenge to play a postal game with *Hitech* (Hans Berliner's well-known computer chess program at Carnegie Mellon University) was declined. Dunne correctly noted that a computer has much less to gain from a three-day time limit than a human does. An extra one or two ply over tournament play does not nearly compensate for the human's use of three days plus the added ability to move the pieces around.

How would a computer affect postal play? Certainly if a human were weak enough, he could just follow the computer's "overnight mode" move suggestion and his play would improve. But for stronger players it is certainly not clear exactly what the current (~1989) computer crop would do in terms of "illegal help" (postal chess organizations forbid computer analysis except for special tournaments) – and certainly not everyone has access to a *Deep Thought*, a *Hitech*, or even a master-level program.

So, out of scientific curiosity, I proposed a "no-rules" fun postal match to Dennis Dunn, an experienced postal player (no relation; different spelling from Alex). The express purpose was to allow me to use a computer to aid my play and to see what would happen. Although I am an inexperienced postal player, as an over-the-board master, a member of the International Computer Chess Association, and a software professional I felt more than adequately qualified. Another principal purpose was to document my experience. After all, everyone is afraid that using computers would ruin postal play because humans would have their moves controlled by computers stronger than they. However, the use of the computer as a "tool" for stronger postal players (who would not just accept a computer move as a substitute for their own) was a somewhat unexplored subject.

For the experiment I chose not to use any "standalone" computers, but rather PC (or in my case Macintosh) programs that I had personally purchased. The reason for this is in the graphic representation of the tree search; I wanted/needed to see the depth and current width parameters as well as the entire tree of current "best move;" the limited display capabilities of the standalones made this view much more cumbersome. Availability was another factor. The relative affordability of PC software made its use more accessible. For example, my company has a 68020-based Macintosh II that I could use after work and on weekends; a comparable 68020 Fidelity Mach IV standalone computer (rated 2325) would cost well over $1000 (and I didn't apply for a grant for this research!).

Most of the PC programs to which I had access were older and certainly weaker than the standalones. However, for the *"Hitech"* reason mentioned in the first paragraph, this lack of strength was not too important to me.

I proposed to Dennis that we play two games, one with each color ("A" and "B"). However, on move 19 of the game in which I had Black a fascinating divergence occurred where I had two continuations that gave up material: a queen sacrifice and an exchange sacrifice. So, I proposed creating a third game, C (Game 25), and Dennis, a good sport throughout, readily accepted.

Before presenting analysis of the games, let my summarize my "lessons learned":

- As could be expected, the computer could be a big help in certain situations, like tactical mêlées; in other positions, however, even letting it run all weekend was no help at all, just as Alex Dunne (and I) predicted. Ironically, some of the best tactical shots (for example 18...♕e5, 23...b4, and 36...♗e6+ in Game 25) were found by me! The computer couldn't see the consequences of such moves because they were just too deep; many involved positional squeezes such as the one Walter Browne put on *Deep Thought* when the latter became the first computer to beat a grandmaster and win a large open tournament in 1988.

- The amount of time I took to use the computers was enormous. The incredible overhead of forcing the computer to look at the various plans I suggested took up gobs of time. Although, as mentioned above, I am not an experienced postal player, I had to take up at least twice the time I would have used normally. I can say this because in certain positions I essentially played as if the computer were not there, anyway (to my great chagrin in Game B, I might add!).

- Because of my experience with computers, artificial intelligence, chess algorithms, etc., I was able to make use of the tree information in a way most postal players could not. I would estimate that many would just accept the computer's move or have the computer verify their move. This blind acceptance and/or tactical verification would be of great help to a weak player, but of little help to a master except in the most confusing of situations. Such a complicated situation occurred only a couple of times, in Game 25.

Conclusion: I agree that computers should not be allowed in postal play, but current computer capabilities would not have a dramatic effect in the majority of positions that would occur at high-level play. For weaker postal players it is no surprise that a computer would have a dramatic effect on the strength of their play, but even a weaker player would do well to double-check moves in the endgame especially, where incredible blunders are possible, even if the computer thinks over a weekend. This kind of blunder could have occurred frequently in some endgame lines that might have been played in Game A.

Dennis Dunn – Dan Heisman
Correspondence Game
Warrington, Penna. 1989
Sicilian Scheveningen

1.e4	c5
2.♘f3	e6
3.d4	cxd4
4.♘xd4	♘f6
5.♘c3	d6
6.♗e2	♘c6

Not the most common idea. Usually a combination of ...♗f8-e7, ...♕d8-c7, and ...a7-a6 is played first.

7.0-0	♗e7
8.♔h1	0-0

For White to play ♔g1-h1 without ever playing ♗c1-e3 is fairly rare.

9.f4	♗d7
10.♘b3	♕c7
11.♗f3	♖fd8
12.♘b5!?	...

The first deviation from known play. A previous game in the *Informant* had gone 12.g4 with complications.

12...	♕b8

13.c4 **a6**

Another slower idea is 13...♗e8 and ... ♘d7-c5.

14.♘c3! **...**

If 14.♘d4(?), Black can break in the center with a timely ...e6-e5 in the near future.

14... **b5**
15.e5?! **...**

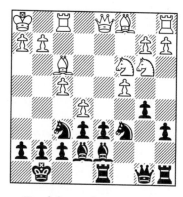

Position after 15.e5?!

This exciting thrust makes games A and C very interesting. White sees the chance to win material. I was expecting the more prosaic 15.♕e2 (15.cxb5? axb5 justifies Black's previous play) 15...bxc4 16.♕xc4 ♘b4! with the threat of ...♖dc8 and then ...♘xa2, e.g. 17.♕e2 ♘xa2 18.♖xa2 ♕xb3 19.♖xa6 ♖xa6 20.♕xa6 =.

15... **dxe5**

Black accepts the challenge. Certainly playable is the more passive 15...♘e8, where White has a comfortable game with nothing to worry about except how to generate a kingside attack.

16.fxe5 **♕xe5**
17.♗f4 **...**

This is White's idea. The black queen has no good squares (17...♕f5? 18.♗c7 winning material for little compensation) and so must take the bishop, giving White a combination winning material.

17... **♕xf4**
18.♗xc6 **...**

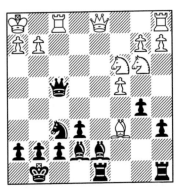

Position after 18.&xc6

Now Black has several decisions to make. He can get three pawns for a piece – and this was the line the computer recommended to me! – by 18...♕xc4 19.♗xa8 ♖xa8 20.♖xf6 ♗xf6 21.♕xd7 ♖d8 22.♕a7 ♗xc3 (22... b4?!) 23.bxc3 ♕xc3 when further analysis shows Black may not be lost, but White is certainly much better.

I really never strongly considered playing the computer's suggestion. The immediate thought that hit me (back when White sent the move 15.e5?!) was to play 18...♕e5 and on 19.♗xa8 ♗d6 threatening mate and then making use of the bishop pair and weak white diagonal. However, at first I didn't like the exchange sacrifice line (from 19...♗d6) 20.g3 ♖xa8 21.cxb5 axb5 22.♕d4, more or less forcing the trade of queens, a line tactically justified because Black can't win a piece by 22...♗c6+ 23.♔g1 ♕xd4 24.♘xd4 ♗c5 25.♘ce2 e5 26.♖fc1 ♘d7 27.b4! and White wins. Then it hit me to play 18...♕xf1+ with a rook, bishop, and pawn for the queen, for if White tries to win back the pawn with 18...♕xf1+ 19.♕xf1 ♗xc6 20.cxb5 axb5 21.♘xb5 ♗xb5 22.♕xb5 ♖xa2! 23.♕e2, Black gets pressure in the endgame.

However, by the time I had to reply to move 18 I had spent quite a bit of time and found an improvement (see Black's move 23) over the exchange sacrifice discussed above, so I proposed to split the game into two: in game A (the original game), I would play 18...♕xf1+ and try to win the endgame, while in game C (the present game), I would play 18...♕e5 with a potentially exciting middlegame. As noted above in the introductory text, Dennis was a very good sport and unconditionally accepted.

The only problem was: what if White plays (after 18...♕e5) 19.♖e1(!) ? Then there could be an immediate draw after 19...♕f4, or Black could try to play a line similar to game A with 19...♕xe1+ where White cannot win back the b-pawn and the bishop pair since the queen no longer covers b5. However, after...

18...   ♕e5

White played instead:

19.♗xa8   ...

Avoiding the more prosaic possibility of 19.♖e1 and the fight was on!

19...   ♗d6

Of course, without this *Zwischenzug* the move 18...♕e5 makes much less sense. White is forced to weaken his long diagonal to prevent mate on h2.

20.g3   ♖xa8
21.cxb5   ...

This is sensible, as it stops the threats of 21...♗c6+ and 21...bxc4 with one move.

21...   axb5
22. ♕d4   ...

This was the move mentioned in the note to White's 18th. However, it is by no means forced; it just forces the trade of queens, which looks good for White. However, as the annotator, I have the obligation to pinpoint the losing move. The possibilities are 15.e5, 19.♗xa8 (instead of 19.♖e1!?), and this move, 22.♕d4. After the game, White (Dennis) wasn't sure, and I'll give a tentative vote that the loser was 15.e5. Getting back to White's 22nd, other moves such as 22.♘d4 are possible. The problem with a move like 22.♘d4 is that, while stopping the immediate threat of 22...♗c6+, it does nothing to slow Black's long-term attack. With two bishops, a pawn, and a weak light-square diagonal to the white king in return for a rook and a knight, it seems that Black has more than enough compensation. This observation was shared by Dennis, and that is why he played 22.♕d4. After 22.♘d4 I was considering several possibilities for continuing the attack. For example, after 22...h5 Black is threatening combinations of ...h5-h4 and ...♘f6-g4.

22...   ♗c6+
23.♔g1   b4!! −+

Position after 23...b4!!

This was the move I had been so desperately searching for when the forcing line began with White's 15th move. Without this move, White's whole concept of 15.e5?! is much sounder. Luckily for me, postal chess is played at a rather slow rate and I was able to find 23...b4!! before I had to make the decisions discussed above following White's 18th move. Rather than the "obvious" 23...♛xd4 24.♘xd4 ♝c5 which, as mentioned in the note to White's 18th, doesn't work, this pawn push contains killer value.

While 23...b4!! took much longer to find (by the point I *had* to find it, White's 18th move) than 16.c4!! in my game with Lunenfeld (Game 24), because one was over-the-board and the other was postal I am equally proud of these two subtle pawn pushes. Without either I would not have been able to realize a winning advantage; in fact, without either I might have lost instead of won, much less drawn.

24.♕xe5   **...**

Forced, as after 24.♘e2 ♕xe2 threatens mate and leaves no time for White to recover his material, and other moves, like 24.♘d1, would lose to 24...♕xd4 25.♘xd4 ♝c5.

24...   **♝xe5**

[A funny story: This game was published in *Chess Life*. I had submitted the game with extensive notes, and shown that at this point I was winning by force. The master who published the column chose to ignore my notes and included very few notes, although around this point of the game he commented that the chances were about even – basically telling me I was wrong, even though computer analysis backed me up! My reaction was one of incredulity – I would certainly have offered to play out this position, giving draw odds, to that master, so long as we could both use computer help. I think I would win every time! At 23 ply after 25.♘d1, *Rybka* has Black rated ahead by 1.16 pawns after 25...h5. That is generally enough to win...]

25.♘d1 ...

Again forced to protect the b-pawn – and then the a-pawn.

25... **♗d5!**

Position after 25...♗d5!

While this move is obvious, its strength is more than meets the eye. Despite being up the exchange for a pawn, White is weak on the a2, b2, b3 and d4 squares and the pin of the a-pawn is not easy to meet. Of course, now 26.♘c1?? ♗d4+ 27.♘f2 ♘g4 wins for Black.

26.♖e1 ...

Despite the reduced material, this is becoming a nice position in which to have a computer on your side. The coming piece play becomes very delicate. I had expected around here 26.♖c1 or 27.♖c1 to guard the a-pawn due to impending back-rank mate, but after Black replies ...♔g8-f8 or maybe even better, ...h7-h5, there is still no defense to the threats on both a2 and b3.

26... **♘g4!**

I must admit, this is the computer's move. It looks risky, but the computer "assured" me of its safety.

27.♘f2 ...

Trying for "removal of the guard." The superficial try 27.h3? fails to 27...♗xg3, when the white rook on e1 is embarrassed.

27...   ♗xb2

And now if 28.♘xg4 ♗xb3 29.♖ab1 ♖xa2, Black's threat of 30...♗d4+ wins easily.

28.♖ad1   ♘e5

The beginning of a recurring theme. Because of the awkward placing of White's pieces, a discovered attack is a constant threat that allows Black to win a tempo here and, a few moves later, essentially paralyzes White's pieces in a manner that would make Nimzowitsch proud.

29.♖e3   ...

Practically forced to stop the threat of 29...♘f3+. Of course, in some lines, Black must be a little careful because now, if the rook leaves the back rank to capture the a-pawn, then ...♘e5-f3+ is met by ♖xf3 and Black cannot play ...♗xf3 because of ♖d8 and mate.

29...   ♘c4!

This is my move, not the computer's. I, of course, first wanted to play 29...♖xa2, but I, more than the computer, was afraid of the sequence 30.♖xd5 exd5 31.♘d3 f6 32.♘xb4 d4! 33.♖xe5 ♖a3 34.♖e7 ♖xb3 35.♘c6 when Black should win but the fun is gone. It seems that I should have more in the position, and indeed 28...♘c4, in hindsight, is clearly better as it keeps up the pressure.

30.♖3d3   ...

Not falling for 30.♖3e1 ♗c3! and Black wins the exchange with continuing pressure. White is shooting for some lines where he exchanges into an endgame with only a rook and two pawns (g,h) versus bishop and five (b,e,f,g,h) or, if White is lucky, bishop and four (e,f,g,h). The bishop and five is probably a win for Black, but it is not so easy because White's king is better placed for the endgame. The bishop and four should be a draw.

30...   ♖xa2

Because now the exchange sacrifice 31.♖xd5 exd5 32.♖xd5 g6 is no big deal for White.

31.♘d4   ...

Again not forced but, as mentioned above, nothing is much better.

31...   **♘e5!**

Once again Black makes use of the tempo-winner. White has nothing better than...

32.♖e3   **...**

32.♖3d2 fails to 32...♗xd4 when Black wins the house after a later ...♘e5-f3+.

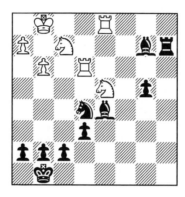

Position after 32.♖e3

32...   **f6!**

Ouch! Black quietly prevents the back-rank mate that he would be faced with after 32...♗xd4? 33.♖xd4 ♘f3+??? 34.♖xf3 ♗xf3? 35.♖d8; after the mate threats are gone, White has no hope.

33.♘e2   **...**

Forced because of the threats of 33...♗xd4 and 34...♘f3+.

33...   **♘f3+**
34.♔g2   **...**

Giving up the h-pawn with 34.♔f1 does not save a tempo since after 34...♘h2+ White cannot gain anything with 35.♔e1 ♘f3+. Dennis agreed with me after the game that this was a torturous position to have to play against a computer!

34...   **♘d4+**
35.♔h3   **...**

Trying for some variance and avoiding an ongoing set of similar threats. I was planning the same reply after 35.♔g1. However, new simplifying combinations now appear because the white king is removed from the main battleground.

35...   **e5**

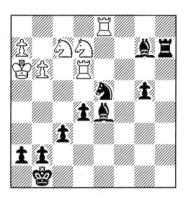

Position after 35...e5

The ultimate triumph for Black. White has absolutely no constructive moves! The computer now suggests 36.g4 for White, which shows you how hopeless White's position has become.

36.♘e4?   **...**

The proverbial "blunder in a lost position." Black can now win the exchange with 36...♘f5, which of course the material-greedy computer loved. However, in that line White can struggle on – and after the game Dennis confirmed that he would not have resigned. However, I thought I might have a better move here. Since I couldn't ask the computer, "What are other possibilities?," I watched the monitor to see on which moves the computer was making alpha-beta cut-offs more slowly. Among these I noticed...

36...   **♗e6+!**

...and with the move I sent the "if" moves, If 37.♔g2 ♗c3 (as played), and if 37.g4 then 37...h5. The latter leads to cute play, for example 37.g4 h5 38.♘f2, and now Black has either 1) 38...hxg4+ 39.♘xg4 f5 40.♘xe5 f4+ 41.♘g4 (forced) 41...fxe3 42.♘xd4 ♗xd4 43.♖xd4 ♗xg4+ 44.♔xg4 e2 45.♖e4 b3 with the unstoppable idea of ...b3-b2-b1; or 2) 38...♖a3 (or 38...hxg4+ first) 39.♖xa3 (forced) 39...bxa3 40.♘c1 hxg4+ 41.♘xg4 ♗xc1 42.♖xc1 a2 with the unstoppable idea of ...♘d4-b3 or ...♘c2.

37.♔g2   **♗c3**

The computer liked 37...♗g4 winning the exchange but, as on the previous move, "What does he know?" After 37...♗c3, White must lose material because of the pin. For example, on 38.♔f2 (or ♔f1) 38...♗c4 or ...♗g4 allows Back to trade everything off with Black up three pawns in a king and pawn (or one piece) endgame.

38.♘xc3   **bxc3**

And now again the same problems apply for White as on the previous move, with ♔&♙ endgame simplification threatened, so...

39.♖xd4   **exd4**
40.♖xe6   **...**

Position after 40.♖xe6

Now of course Black can get fancy and play 40...♖xe2+ 41.♖xe2 d3 or even the superior 40...d3 41.♔f3 ♖xe2 42.♖xe2 c2 which loosens the h-pawn (for the ensuing queen vs. rook endgame), but in either case with an easy win. However, king-and-pawn endgames are even easier than queen vs. rook, so I sent...

40...   **♔f7**

...and included for Dennis a couple of lines showing Black winning easily in all variations, the principal one being 41.♖e4 d3 42.♔f3 ♖xe2 43.♖xe2 dxe2 44.♔xe2 ♔e6 45.♔d3 ♔f5 46.h3 c2 47.♔xc2 ♔e4, and so...

0-1

In case you are curious, Black also won the "A" game in which the queen sacrifice 18...♕xf1+ was played, but not without some help from

White. In the "B" game, I lost a piece without asking the computer for its analysis(!); the game, while lost for many moves, was finally drawn in a very instructive king, bishop and two pawns vs. king and four pawns endgame. In neither game did there occur the complicated tactical positions in which a computer could greatly help a strong postal player. Most of the moves in all games (including some of the cutest in the "C" game) were made by me. The computer just verified my analysis (especially after I lost the piece in a seemingly calm postion in game "B"!), and this was very time-consuming.

Would I do this again? I guess so, but not just for fun. To do it correctly just takes too much time. If I want to play postal chess in the future, I will gladly do so without the "burden" of the computer – and maybe I can even play in a real postal match!

A Position Worthy of Study

The following position, from a 1992 simultaneous against Edwin Santiago (Black) at a Huntingdon Valley Chess Society Juniors meeting, is worthy of study due to the numerous tactical motifs.

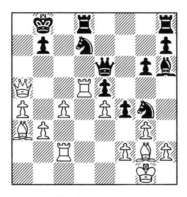

Black to move

Black must stop White's threatened ♗a3-d6+. I thought my piece sacrifice on d5 the previous move had been very speculative and probably unsound, but my analysis (with computer help) showed my position to be won. Black has three main defenses: A) 1... ♘b6?, B) 1...b6, and C) 1... ♕a6. (Note to novices: the "obvious" defenses 1...♘7f6?? and 1...♗f8?? lose the rook on d8.)

A) 1...♘b6? is nicely refuted: 2.♗c5! when 2....♔c7 is not possible due to 3.♗xb6+ ♕xb6 4.♖c5+ winning the queen, and if 2...♖xd5 3.cxd5 and the e6-queen and b6-knight are both attacked. Finally, 2...♘xd5 loses nicely to 3.♗a7+ ♔c8 (3...♔a8 4.♗b6+ ♔b8 5.♕a7+ ♔c8 6.cxd5+ is no better) 4.cxd5+.

B) 1...b6 forces 2.♕a6, but the threat c4-c5xb6 is deadly, e.g.

B1) 2...fxg3 3.c5! and cxb6 cannot be stopped.
B2) Similarly, after 2...♗f8 3.c5! forces Black to sacrifice a piece on c5 to prevent cxb6, and after 3...♗xc5 4.♗xc5 ♘xc5 White wins safely with 5.♖cxc5 △ ♖b5 and a5, but more aggressive is 5.♖dxc5! ♖d1+ 6.♗f1 fxg3 7.hxg3 ♖xf1+!? 8.♔xf1 ♘e3+ 9.fxe3 where ...♕h3+ followed by an

189

eventual ...bxc5 regains the rook but White still wins, in some lines mating with ♕b6+ ♚a8, ♖xc5 △ ♖a5 mate. If Black doesn't play the 7...♖xf1!? fireworks, White gets in ♖b5 and a5 or just ♖c7 with a winning attack.

B3) 2...♘7f6 leads to spectacular play good for White after 3. c5!?, e.g. 3...♘xd5 4.exd5 ♕c8 (other moves lose to 5.c6 with threats of c6-c7 and ♕b7 mate) 5.♕xb6+ ♕b7 and now White, down a rook, can even trade queens with 6.♕xb7+ ♚xb7 as the two bishops + rook backing the four connected passed pawns seem to win easily:

Position after 6...♚xb7 (analysis)

After 7.c6+ ♚a7 8.d6 and White will win material. I have played out this ending with computer help and White won rather easily against all defensive tries. In many lines Black tried to stop queening by putting a rook on c8 and giving up the exchange after ♗g2-h3 and a later ♗xc8, but lost quickly to the advancing pawn mass even though still (temporarily) up a piece.

C) 1... ♕a6. During the game I thought this was a likely defense. But after 2. ♗d6+ ♚a7 (forced because if 2...♚a8 then 3.♗c7! just wins material) White has the pleasant choice of:

C1) 3.♗c7 b6 (the defense not possible after 2...♚a8) 4.♕xa6+ ♚xa6 5.♗xd8 ♖xd8, and the extra pawns and pin on the d-file give White a winning position but, since this line represents one of Black's best chances, perhaps even better for White is:

C2) 3.♕c7 (threatening ♖d5-a5) 3...♖c8! 4.♕xd7 ♘f6 5.♕e6! ♘xd5 6.exd5! when any pin on the d6-bishop can be met by c4-c5. In a computer-vs.-computer playout from this position, White won rather quickly.

There is a little more, but these are the main ideas and I found these to be very pretty.

Game 26

I Get a FIDE Rating

A fter not having played tournament chess for eight years, I came out of retirement with the goal of obtaining a FIDE rating. In my first tournament back, a Pennsylvania State Chess Federation (PSCF) Futurity (Autumn 1989), my first round opponent was Dr. Orest Popovych, and he nicely showed me how rusty I was! With a final score in that tournament of 4-7, I did not get my FIDE rating. Six months later I was in better shape and playing in my second PSCF Futurity. Going into the tenth round I was not only close to a FIDE rating, but also in contention with Dr. Popovych for a prize. Since getting a draw would help me greatly toward my goal, I was not necessarily playing for a win. However, Dr. Popovych is a great fighter and peace wasn't on his mind.

Heisman (2201; FIDE Unr.) – Popovych (2377; FIDE 2275)
PSCF Futurity
Warminster, Penna. 1990
English Opening
(40 moves in 2 hours)

1.e4!   **...**

The exclamation point is for the transposition, which got the opening I wanted, but did not faze Dr. Popovych one bit.

1...	**c5**
2.c4	**♘c6**
3.♘c3	**g6**
4.g3	**♗g7**
5.♗g2	**d6**
6.♘1e2	**♘f6**
7.O-O	**O-O**
8.d3 (1)	**♗d7**

[This setup for White is called the Botvinnik Variation. Many years after this game was played, GM Tony Kosten wrote a book called *The Dynamic English*, where he suggested that the Botvinnik was not as effective in the Symmetrical English (1.c4 c5) as it is against ...e5 defenses like 1.c4 e5 2.g3 g6 3.♗g2 ♗g7. It is therefore consistent with

GM Kosten's suggestion that my choice of variation in this game is not the most accurate. If it were, then anyone could choose to play this way with effect against the Sicilian, as I tried to do here.]

9.h3	♘e8
10.♗e3 (9)	♘d4
11.♖b1 (12)	a5
12.♔h2 (20)	♗c6
13.f4 (21.5)	f5 (2)

So much for my opening finesse. At this point I had used over 20 minutes, Dr. Popovych 2!

14.♗g1 (25)	e5! (6)
15.exf5?! (33)	...

[*Rybka* prefers 15.fxe5 dxe5 16.exf5 gxf5 17.♘d5, with an almost equal game.]

15...	♗xg2
16.♔xg2 (33)	gxf5 (14)
17.♘d5 (36)	♘c7 (20)
18.♘2c3 (41)	♘7e6
19.♗e3 (43)	...

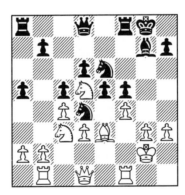

Position after 19.♗e3

Black has full equality with a sort of knight-dance stalemate in the center. I offered a draw, but Black has visions of attack along the g-file, so...

19...	♔h8 (23)
20.♖f2 (51)	...

To protect the c2 square next move.

20...   ♖g8
21.♕h5!? (57)   ...

A double-edged move, preventing ideas like ...♗g7-h6 and ...♗f6, but limiting the queen's mobility and thus increasing her vulnerability. And now, for the first time, Dr. Popovych seemed to really start thinking (not that he was worried).

21...   ♕d7 (42)
22.♕h4 (66.5)   ...

22.♘b6 fails to ...♕c6+, a recurring theme hereabouts.

22...   ♖af8 (49)

Preventing knight incursions.

23.♔h2 (69.5)   ♖f7

Guarding e7.

24.♖1f1 (71)   **b5!** (63)

The best attempt to win. Black has a slight initiative now. However, it should be noted that if Black did nothing it would be almost impossible for White to make progress.

25.b3 (82)   **b4** (66)
26.♘e2 (83.5)   **e4?!**

Dr. Popovych, true to his style, plays aggressively. From a psychological standpoint, it is also a good move, for he has considerably more time left; I have used 70% of my time and the complications are just starting! His move wins the exchange, but it was difficult to see that it was too soon. Black should prepare this move to prevent what occurred in the game.

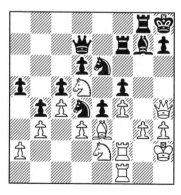

Position after 26...e4?!

27.dxe4 (86)   **fxe4** (75)
28.f5! (89)   **...**

I defend actively. Probably a passive defense was possible, but 28.f5 seemed a natural way to gain space and activate my pieces more than his.

28...   ♘f3+

One advantage to 28.f5 is that there is no going back for Black; if he first retreats the knight on e6, then simply 29.♕xe4 leaves White up a pawn and winning.

29.♖xf3 (89.5)   **exf3**

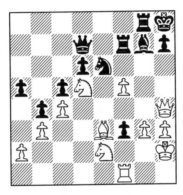

Position after 29...exf3

30.fxe6! (103.5)   **...**

I took almost half my remaining time for this move. My original intention was to grab the f-pawn and capture the black knight when it landed on d4: 30.♖xf3 ♘d4 31.♗xd4 cxd4 32.♘xd4 to hold the f-pawn. However, the complications of the text intrigued me. After the game I couldn't wait to go home and give this (and the forthcoming) complicated positions to my chess computer, since those little things are real good at this type of piece interplay. Usually with this amount of complications, the computer is much better and finds big holes in the actual play (as seen in many of the other complicated positions in this book), but amazingly the computer confirmed my play for this and the next couple of moves, even though time was running short. I was especially tempted by the continuation 30.fxe6 fxe2 31.♖xf7 ♕xe6 32.♘f6?! threatening mate, since Black has few mate defenses: the tries 32...♕xf7?? 33.♕h7# and 32...♗xf6?? 33.♕h7# were all I saw at this point.

30...   **fxe2**

These two consecutive "30.fxe" moves are not the normal pawn recaptures! Black has little choice but to try a queening combination.

31.♖xf7 (104)   **♕xe6** (81)

All as planned. Unfortunately, now I saw that 32.♘f6 fails to 32...♕xf6!, so I had to look for an alternative idea. Later the computer suggested 32.♖xg7!? to threaten mate and retain two pieces for the rook. However, after 32...♖xg7 33.g4 ♕e5+ 34.♔g2, the computer also found 34...♕b2! 35.♕e1 (forced) and after 35...♕xa2 or similar, Black has good counterchances. Meanwhile the spectators (primarily the other masters in the Futurity) were having fun following the game's complicated position.

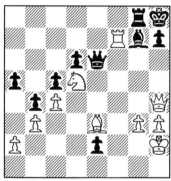

Position after 31.♕xe6

32.♖e7!? (110.5)   **♕xd5**

Forced. Unfortunately for Black, he cannot try to win the exchange with 32...♕xe7?? because after 33.♘xe7 e1♕ he loses nicely to 34. ♘g6#!

[*Rybka* says that Black should bail out with 32...e1♕ 33.♖xe6 ♕e2+ 34.♔h1 ♕e1+, draw.]

33.cxd5   **e1♕**

So after all that the material is dead even!

34.♕e4 (115.5)   **...**

Tying down the bishop to shield the h7 square. At this point I only have a few minutes left to get to move 40, while Dr. Popovych has over half an hour.

34...   **♕e2+** (90)

[*R:* This may be the losing move! Much better is 34...♕a1 with rough equality, e.g. 35.♕c2 ♕c3! =.]

35.♕g2 (116.5)   ...

I'm still happy to get that vital half-point, even though I may be better here.

35...   **♕xg2+?** (90)

This, however, may be close to losing. Keeping the queens on the board gives Black better chances, especially since I have about three minutes to make five moves and Dr. Popovych has 30!

[*R*: Other tries, like 35...♕d1 or 35...♕e1 are not much better, so 35...♕xg2+ does not deserve a question mark. The damage was done on Black's 34th move.]

36.♔xg2 (116.5)   **♗e5**

Superficially, it looks like Black is O.K.

37.g4 (117)   **h5**
38.♔f3   ...

White's play is all forced but, being short of time, that is O.K. with me as long as my forced moves don't lead to a bad position. Often these "reduced flexibility" positions are bad; here it is not.

38...   **hxg4+**
39.hxg4 (117)   **♖f8+**
40.♔e4! (119.5)   ...

Position after 40.♔e4!

I took two-and-a-half of my remaining three minutes to decide between this active move and 40.♔e2, preventing the black rook from penetrating. But, now that the smoke has cleared at time control and, despite his weaker pawn structure, White is ahead. He has a stronger, centralized king and the double threats of 41.♖a7 winning the a-pawn and 41.♗xc5, also winning a pawn. White's king is also protected from the threat I was concerned about, 40...♖f1, 41...♖e1, and 42...♗d4, because of the simple 40...♖f1 41.♗xc5 ♖e1+ 42.♔f5 (or even 42.♗e3). So, in view of White's threats, it is no wonder Black tries to rid himself of one of his weaknesses:

40...   a4?!

[*R:* Clearly 40...a4 loses, so Black had to try 40...♔g8 or 40...♗h2, when White is clearly better but no immediate win is on the horizon.]

41.♖xe5!   ...

My first move past time control is no mistake! At first, when considering my move, I didn't fully anticipate the strength of this continuation. 41.♖xe5! strikes me as the type of move which a strong player would hardly ever miss, but a weaker player is sometimes afraid to play. Strangely enough, if you gave the weaker player a "White to play and win" problem, then they, too, would correctly find the first move of this combination.

41...   dxe5
42.♗xc5   axb3

So that 43.♗xf8?? b2 wins for Black!

43.axb3   ♖e8

What else is Black to do? White has too many targets and his king's position is deadly. If 43..♖f4+ 44.♔xe5 ♖xg4, then 45.d6 is unstoppable.

44.d6! (133)   ...

White needs tempi, not pawns. Now I saw the winning line 44...♔g7 45.♔d5 ♔f6 46.d7 ♖d8, 47.♔d6 threatens 48.♗b6 – but Dr. Popovych saw the even faster 44...♔g7 45.♗b6! when 45...♖d8 46.♔xe5 ♔g7 47.♔e6 is easy, so...

1-0

Eventually I finished 7-4, in third place, while Dr. Popovych fourth with 6.5-4.5, so this game helped me win a prize. More importantly, I then had the pleasant problem of determining whether I had enough total games to qualify for a FIDE rating. My FIDE rating performance result of about 2300 was certainly above the minimum needed of 2205!

If I get the rating and thus attain my goal, then maybe I can return to a peaceful retirement. A new goal would be to help protégé Danny Benjamin get his FIDE rating at a younger age than I was when I started playing in rated tournaments (16). He should make it. Or maybe I should look for another personal goal...

Note: For my performance in this tournament I received a FIDE rating of 2285, which placed me in a tie with GM Arnold Denker for 199th on the U.S. FIDE list. My name and rating first appeared in *Informant 49*, page 437 [now always at http://ratings.fide.com/card.phtml?event=2002299]. I would like to thank Danny, IM Bruce Rind, and Arthur Mitchell for their role in preparing me for this tournament and helping me achieve my goal.

Once I started annotating my games, I never stopped. I tried to be objective by showing my notes to friends and, later, testing the notes via computer. It is more difficult for a player starting chess at sixteen to become a strong player than for one starting earlier, most likely between the ages of seven through eleven. I believe that annotating my games played helped me to overcome some of this age handicap, and played a meaningful part in eventually improving my game to the master level. I hope the reader gives annotation a try and finds it just as worthwhile.

Game 27

In Pursuit of the Main Line Chess Club Championship

The following game was played in the final round of the 2003 Main Line Chess Club Championship. I was tied for first place with a former student, Expert Mike Glick. The game was played at a time limit of game in 75 minutes (G/75) without time delay – bad for the old guy, but I did not have a digital clock available. Time *remaining* is in parentheses.

Dan Heisman (2224) – Joe Mucerino (2084)
Main Line CC Championship (Round 5)
Gladwyne, Penna. 2003
English Opening

1.c4	e5
2.g3	♘f6
3.♗g2	d6

An unusual move order. I could not see anything special for White, so I played a Botvinnik setup.

4.♘c3	g6
5.e4	♗g7
6.♘1e2	O-O
7.O-O	♘c6
8.f4 (72 min. left)	...

So far, so book, although apparently Joe was just playing natural moves.

8...	♗e6 (69)
9.d3	♘e8?

Not the right idea in this position. Best is 9...♕d7 preventing 10.f5, which would become an "interesting" sacrifice.

10.f5 (70.5)	♗d7 (66.5)
11.♘d5 (68)	♘d4? (64)

199

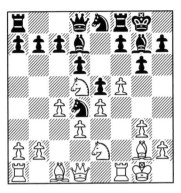

Position after 11...♘d4?

This is likely the losing move. Even the ugly 11...f6 is much better. It is interesting how us mortals often make losing moves much earlier than they do in the books! After the move 11.♘d5 I knew I was threatening to play f5-f6 in many variations and now Joe has allowed just that. In all the lines but one it won easily. But what to do about that one line? In that line Joe sacrifices his queen for some very interesting counterplay.

12.♘xd4 (65)   **...**

Just to prevent some ideas around the square g4, and simplify.

12...   **exd4**

Finally I saw an idea of how I could still get the advantage after the queen sacrifice, and so the next few moves proceeded rather rapidly.

13.f6! (61.5)   **♘xf6** (58)

Forced. ♖esignation follows 13...♗h8?? 14.♘e7+ winning the house and 13...♗xf6? 14.♘xf6 ♘xf6 15.♗g5.

14.♗g5   **...**

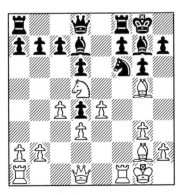

Position after 14.♗g5

14...   ♘xd5!

Again forced. Interesting, when I showed this position to some mid-1000s students, they never seriously considered this move (at least without help), which Joe played instantly. To a large extent, this fear of sacrifice in real positions – as opposed to problems – shows a main tactical difference between a 1500 and a 2000!

15.♗xd8 (61)   ♘e3 (58)

So far, so forced, but what now? White has pieces hanging all over the place, but of course giving back the queen is not a possibility, so moving the queen is forced, but where? This is the decision I had to make when deciding to push f5-f6, around move 12. If I settle for the centralizing 16.♕e2, then after 16...♖axd8 Black has a lot of compensation for his queen. Note that the greedy 16...♘xf1 17.♗xc7 is even worse for Black. Instead of getting a piece, he gets a rook for two pawns, which is not nearly as good! Weak players make terrible counting errors in positions like these. Which brings up an important point: I recently hosted IM [now GM] Larry Kaufman's famous article *The Evaluation of Material Imbalances* on my website, www.danheisman.com. For serious players who missed this award-winner in the March 1999 *Chess Life*, catch it now!

16.♕b3!   ...

This is it – the destruction of Black's queenside is more important than saving the exchange (on the next move). Once I found this move, my evaluation was that I was theoretically winning, which is why 11... ♘d4 is likely the losing move.

16...   ♖fxd8 (55.5)

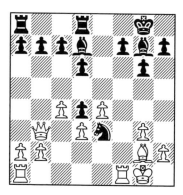

Position after 16...♖fxd8

17.♕xb7!   **...**

Fritz likes this only slightly better than 17.♖f2, but beginners would hardly consider 17.♕xb7 at all since "they would lose a rook." Nonsense. They would only be losing the exchange, and a weak rook for a very strong knight. After 17.♖f2 b6 I bet I would have had a much more difficult time winning the game!

17...   **c5**

Joe also realizes that keeping his queenside in one piece is more important than winning the exchange. But he is overdoing it. *Fritz* (and I) think he should have grabbed the exchange with 17...♘xf1 when still White is much better, likely winning. However, after the text I can guard b2 and prepare some timely exchange sacrifice(s).

18.♖f2 (53)   **♗e6 (46)**

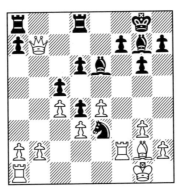

Position after 18...♗e6

Weaker players would tend to think this position would win itself with my advantage of queen for two bishops. But without open lines my rooks are fairly worthless, so my plan here is to make two sacrifices: first a pawn to open lines for my bishop, and then the exchange (hopefully for a pawn, too) to open a decisive line for my rooks.

19.e5 (47)   **...**

At six minutes, one of my slowest moves of the game. *Fritz* likes 19.b4!? here, but I don't know how to play that kind of chess! Now I may be even threatening to play ♕xa8. Joe makes the practical decision of taking the pawn and the bishop pair and blockade!

19...   **♘xg2 (42)**
20.♔xg2   **♗xe5**
21.♖e1 (42)   **...**

So that on 21...f6, 22.♖xf6! is decisive.

21...   **♖e8 (33)**
22.b3 (30.5)   **a5 (33)**
23.♖1f1 (36.5)   **...**

So now the exchange target switches to f7, but what to do about the potential perpetual attacks to the queen along the seventh rank? Once I play ♖xf7, I can't just move my queen anywhere, so I have to be careful.

23...   **♖ab8(?)**

This makes things a lot easier, as I gain a tempo by attacking f7 and a5. I would really have to work after the better 23...♖eb8 or possibly 23....f5?!.

24.♕c7 (36)   **♖a8**

There is nothing better.

25.♖xf7 (40)   **...**

It is important to note that I took six of my remaining 36 minutes to make this breakthrough. So many of my students see what they think is a decisive sacrificial line and then play it quickly, often overlooking a line that refutes it completely. If you play a move that you think wins (and is sharp), you have to take your time because you are betting the entire game that you are right, so you certainly want to know if you might be wrong! This is just good time management. What am I going to do with the extra time at the end of the game anyway? So now the question is, what does White do if Black attacks his queen forever?

25...   **♖ac8**

And the answer is...

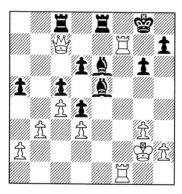

Position after 25...♖ac8

26.♖e7! (29)   ...

A move that most intermediate players would not even consider, *Fritz* says this is best. Joe said he was expecting the simple 26.♕b7 ♖b8 27.♕f3, which is also adequate. (Note: I know what Joe was expecting because, like most of my games, *I reviewed it with my opponent immediately thereafter.* This is a very important habit to develop if you want to improve!)

26...   **♗d5+(?)**

I have to admit, I did not even consider this move – I had considered 26...♗h3+. While it looks like this move is superficially attractive – it doubles and isolates my pawns for a bishop that he is going to lose anyway after 26...♖xc7 27.♖xe8+ ♔g7 28.♖xe6 – it does something far worse: it loses a tempo over that line! In the opening of the game a tempo is worth about a third of a pawn, but later in the game it is usually worth much more (or possibly even less). Don't believe me? Just give someone the odds of an extra tempo anywhere they wish during the game!

27.cxd5   **♖xc7**
28.♖xe8+   **♔g7** (20)
29.♖a8 (26.5)   ...

Now the extra tempo allows me to win the a-pawn, giving me a strong passed a-pawn to boot. Black's only counterplay, down the e-file, is easily nullified after 29...♖e7 30.♖e1!. When you are winning, *Think Defense First* but that does not mean to play passively. So **1-0**.

Meanwhile, Mike Glick was grinding down Vinko Rutar in the endgame. The Main Line CC does not want co-champions, but all four of the tiebreaks between Mike and I were even (draw in the first round!), even cumulative. So, after much deliberation, the club offered us a playoff; we took the title of co-champion and played off for the first and second place prizes. Mike won both games (don't ask!) and deservedly took home the first place Silver Plate. Both our names will be engraved on the club champion list.

Game 28

Winning the Title Outright With a Perfect Score

Three years later I had my chance to get my name on the "Main Line Chess Club Champions" plaque all by itself. This time the game was played at a time limit of game in 70 minutes with a five-second delay.

Vinko Rutar (2150) – Dan Heisman (2224)
Main Line CC Championship
Gladwyne, Penna. 2006
Queen's Pawn Opening

1.d4	♘f6
2.g3	g6
3.♗g2	♗g7
4.c3	...

This move is very unusual. I think Vinko thought that I knew the main book lines better than he did, so he wanted to play something "Reasonable but not book."

4...	O-O
5.♕c2 (69 min. left)	d6 (68.5)
6.♘d2	e5 (66)
7.♘gf3 (67)	♖e8(?) (64.75)

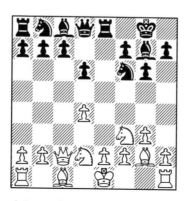

Position after 8...♖e8 (analysis)

I miss my chance! *Rybka* points out that much better is 7...exd4! first and after 8.cxd4 then 8...♖e8 and White finds it awkward to easily develop. For example, if White tries 9.♘c4 ♘c6 10.0-0 ♗f5 11.♕d1 ♕d7 12.♘e3 then Black is slightly better.

8.dxe5	**dxe5** (64.5)
9.e4 (66)	**c6** (62)

Slightly better is 9...♘bd7.

10.O-O	**♕c7** (60.5)
11.b3	**♗e6** (59)

Rybka thinks 11...♘a6 is more accurate, when Black is about even. I don't mind allowing the knight to hit the bishop. In that event, both sides will end up taking exactly two tempos to re-establish their pieces back to the same squares...and that's what happened!

12.♘g5	**♗c8** (58)

Black of course will not give White the bishop pair that easily! Allowing 13.♘xe6 would be a clear inaccuracy.

13.♗a3	**h6** (58)

To clear the way for the return of the bishop, of course.

14.♘gf3	**♗e6** (57.5)

Presto! See the previous note.

15.♖fd1	**♘a6** (56.5)
16.♘f1	**♖ad8** (56)
17.♘e3	**♘g4** (54.5)

Best. *Rybka* now expects us to continue 18.♘xg4 ♗xg4 19.h3 ♗e6...

18.♘xg4 (58.5)	**♗xg4** (54.5)
19.h3	**♗e6** (53.5)

...with equality!

20.♔h2	**c5!** = (47)

Best again. Black neutralizes the bishop on a3.

21.♘d2	**...**

Rybka's number one move! So at this point in the game Vinko and I get some credit for finding the right ideas – that's not always true when masters and experts play. ☺

21...	**b5** (41)

21...♞b8 is slightly more accurate. Now with perfect play White may be able to get a slight advantage.

22.♗f1 (52.5) ...

More accurate is 22.♞f1. Play might continue 22...♛a5 23.♗b2 with a very minor advantage for White.

22... ♛**b6** (39)

I saw but misevaluated the very good and consistent line 22...c4 23.bxc4 bxc4 24.♛a4 ♞c5 25.♛b5 ♞d3 ∓.

23.c4 (51.5) **b4** (38.5)
24.♗b2 ♞**b8** ∓ (36.5)

Up to now the game has featured a lot of maneuvering. Vinko has played very quickly and I have tried not to fall too far behind (not that keeping up with your opponent is important, but falling too far behind a strong player can be dangerous). But the maneuvering pretty much will stop here as the game takes a much sharper turn, starting with White's mistake on the next move. Patience is sometimes a virtue in chess...

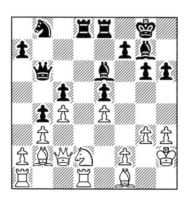

Position after 24...♞b8

25.f4? (49.5) ...

...but perhaps Vinko was growing impatient. Break moves are supposed to open lines for *your* pieces, and here it is Black's army, not White's, which is better able to take advantage of the opening of the position. For example, the opening of the h2-b8 diagonal to the white king allows potential pins. Better is 25.♞f3, 25.♔g1, or 25.♗g2, waiting, when Black is some advantage, but there's no clear way to break through soon.

25... **exf4**
26.gxf4 ♛**c7**

Making the strong pin. Even slightly better is 26...♗xb2 27.♕xb2 ♖d4 and Black is clearly on top.

27.e5

If 27.♔g3, then 27...g5 just makes things worse.

27...   ♗**f5!** (25.5)
28.♘e4   ...

I was expecting 28.♕c1, when *Rybka* suggests either 28...♘d7 or 28...♘c6 with a nice Black edge.

28...   **f6!** ∓ (22)

Putting my finger on the weak white center. Weaker players are often overly cautious about making pawn moves like this in front of their king, but stronger players understand that if it gives them the advantage then subsequent king safety issues should be resolved in their favor.

29.♖xd8 (44)   ...

White is faced with a choice of evils. If 29.♖d5 fxe5 30.♗d3, then 30...exf4 31.♗xg7 ♕xg7 32.♖g1 ♖xd5 33.cxd5 g5 34.♘d6 ♗xd3 35.♕xd3 ♖e3 is good for Black. And if 29.♖d6 ♗xe4 30.♕xe4 (30.♖xd8 ♗xc2 31.♖xe8+ ♔f7 −+) 30...♕xd6 wins (but not 30...♖xd6?? 31.exd6 and White survives).

29...   ♖**xd8** (20.5)

I have less than half of the time of my opponent but just about a winning position. If I can keep it that way for a few more moves, the smoke will start to clear and my deficit in time will be rather meaningless.

30.♗g2 (35)   **fxe5** −+ (20.5)

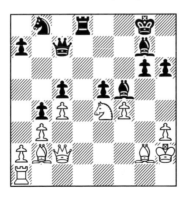

Position after 30...fxe5

So my accurate move order in the past few moves has won a pawn. Unfortunately in the complications over the next few moves I manage to find the second-best choice consistently, throwing away my hard-earned advantage!

31.♖d1 (32)   ...

Best was 31.fxe5, when after 31...♘c6 Black should be able to pocket the win with accurate play.

31...   **♘c6(?)** (18)

Ah, but after 31.♖d1, 31...♘c6 is not the most accurate. I was perplexed in trying to find the right move order, which is tricky. I have lots of flexibility, which is good but can sometimes present too many enticing choices. I should have first played 31...exf4! when after 32.♖xd8+ ♕xd8 33.♗xg7 ♔xg7 34.♕f2 ♗xe4 35.♗xe4 ♕d6 and Black is winning.

32.♖xd8+   **♕xd8?** (16.5)

"Oh for Two"! Again I take time, in this case to decide between the pros and cons of two recaptures – and choose the inferior one! Correct is 32...♘xd8 still maintaining a decisive advantage, e.g. 33.♕d2 exf4 34.♗xg7 ♔xg7 35.♘d6 ♔h7, or 33.fxe5 ♗xe5+ 34.♔h1 ♘e6.

33.♕f2!   ...

Vinko takes full advantage of his opportunity to cause me problems. Now, for the third move in a row, I have to take some time (5 of my remaining 16.5 minutes!) and calculate the multiple possibilities. This time I succeed in finding the only move which still gives me serious chances to win.

33...   **exf4!** (11.5)
34.♗xg7 (26.5)   **♔xg7** (11.5)

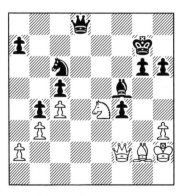

Position after 34...♔xg7

This turns out to be the most crucial decision in a game full of interesting and difficult choices. White has to decide which way to

209

capture: 35.♕xc5, 35.♘xc5, or 35.♕xf4. Vinko chose the most aggressive-looking move, but it turned out to be the final mistake.

35.♕xc5?   **...**

Correct was 35.♕xf4 when the knight on c6 may get to d4, but its base on c5 is still under attack by the white knight and Black's advantage may not be decisive, e.g. 35.♕xf4 ♕e7 (35...♗xe4 is also reasonable; after 36.♗xe4 ♕b8 37.♔g3 ♘e5 Black has winning chances) 36.♘xc5 ♕xc5 37.♕c7+ ♔f6 38.♔h1! Black is much better, but White is still in the game.

35...   **♗xe4! (9.5)**
36.♗xe4   **♕d2+ (9.5)**

A nasty surprise based on some beautiful chess geometry:

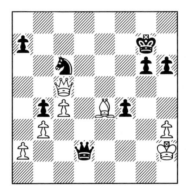

Position after 36...♕d2+

White is strangely helpless, thanks to the flexibility of the knight and its coordination with the queen. If 37.♔h1 (as played in the game) or 37.♔g1, then 37...♕e1+ picks up the bishop *and* guards the knight. But the most beautiful line is 37.♗g2 f3!:

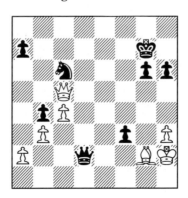

Position after 37...f3 (analysis)

White cannot take the knight with 38.♕xc6? because the f-pawn shields the queen defending against 38...♕xg2#. Notice how the invulnerable knight flexibly defends against all the possible queen checks, such as 38.♘xa7+, 38.♘e5+, or 38.♘e7+. So in this case my wonderfully coordinated forces uphold the principle that *queen and knight usually are superior to queen and bishop.*

37.♔h1 (21.5)	**♕e1+**
38.♔h2	**♕xe4**

With the bishop in my pocket, the win is easy, but I am in mild time pressure, so Vinko understandably makes me show some technique.

39.♕d6	**f3**
40.♕d7+	**♘e7**
41.♔g3	**f2** (6)

I am down to six minutes, but that is plenty of time for me in a position like this.

42.♕d1	**...**

Of course Vinko avoids 42.♔xf2 ♕f5+ trading queens. I am simply trying to force White into a position where when we trade queens the c-pawn will never be a factor. It was not really that difficult – just took a little care on each move, as always.

42...	**♘f5+**
43.♔xf2	**♕f4+**
44.♔e1	**♕e3+**
45.♔f1	**♕xh3+**
46.♔f2	**♕h2+**
47.♔e1	**♕g1+**
0–1	

Eventually I finished this tournament 5-0, winning the club championship outright for the first time and with a performance rating of over 2400. One of my best results! Not bad for age 56, but I don't think Korchnoi has to worry...

Rybka Redux

In the first edition of this book, the three most analytical games were the ones against Yehl, Latzel, and Dowling. Despite having spent many hours analyzing those games, a much better job can be done by any computer today in milliseconds. The Dowling game has already been re-analyzed in the Appendix to the 4th edition of *Elements of Positional Evaluation*.

Let's re-do the analysis of the Yehl and Latzel games with World Computer Champion *Rybka* (rated about 3100+ on my computer) leading the way... to save space I won't repeat all the same text (for the fun of reading that, refer back to the originally annotated games) – I will just re-do the analysis based primarily on what the computer thinks was really happening. Computer evaluations will be given in pawns and ply; for example (0.56/14) means *Rybka* thinks White is better by 56/100 of a pawn at 14 ply.

Game 10: My Best Game

John Yehl (1951) – Dan Heisman (1716)
Keystone State Tournament, Philadelphia 1968
Sicilian Defense

1.e4	c5
2.d4	e6

A spur-of-the-moment decision. I knew that 2...♘f6 and 2...d5 were the main moves (these days 2...g6 and a later ...d7-d5 are also played) but I wanted to keep sparring for opening type.

3.♘f3 ...

White opts for a Sicilian. He could go for a Benoni-type formation with 3.d5.

3... d5

The Marshall Variation, supposedly weak because Black prematurely opens up his game and saddles himself with an isolated d-pawn.

4.dxc5(?) ...

White chooses to isolate the pawn immediately. Instead *Rybka* thinks that the book 4.exd5 is very good for White. After 4...exd5 it gives 5.♗b5+ with a big advantage (0.72; 14).

4...	♗xc5
5.exd5	**exd5**

In this line White's plus is only 0.15 after 6.♗d3, about a normal advantage.

6.♗b5+	**♘c6**

Rybka has this move as clearly best when Black is slighly better. I thought a long time on this move. 6...♗d7 7.♕xd5 ♗xb5 8.♕xc5 does not seem sound for Black and 6...♘d7 is obviously worse.

7.O-O	**♘e7**

I thought this was very necessary and that on 7...♘f6, 8.♖e1+ becomes embarrassing as the pin with development ♗c1-g5 is very strong for White. However, the silicon thinker disagrees and says that after 7...♘f6 8.♕e2+ ♗e6 is the principal variation with Black slightly better, and that on the feared 8.♖e1+ ♗e6 Black is slightly better, e.g. 9.♘g5 O-O! and if 10.♘xe6?! fxe6 11.♖xe6? then 11...♗xf2+ −+. Play might continue 12.♔xf2? ♘e4+ 13.♔e2 ♕h4 and White can resign. So actually 7...♘f6 is best!

8.♘c3	**...**

In the original I gave this move a "(?)" and wrote, "The text is poor. The Knight belongs on d2 after the development of the queen's bishop. It also should protect the king's knight,which will be pinned to the queen by Black's next move, ...♗c8-g4." However, *Rybka* thinks 8.♘c3 is about equal best, along with 8.♗f4. In both cases White is very slightly better.

8...	**♗g4**

Rybka likes 8...♗e6 better.

9.♖e1	**...**

White now threatens the d-pawn by simply 10.♕xd5 or 10.♘xd5. However, this is again slightly inaccurate. *Rybka* prefers either 9.h3 or 9.♗f4 with some pull.

9...	**O-O**

Unpinning the knight protects the d-pawn. The computer confirms that after 9...d4 10.♘e4 is very strong for White and the d-pawn becomes fatally weak. After 9...O-O the game is almost even.

10.♗d3	**...**

The beginning of trouble. White moves the bishop a second time before completing his development. His threat is now 11.♗xh7+ ♔xh7 12.♘g5+ regaining the piece with a pawn and interest. Best is 10.♗e2 with about equal play (-0.01; 13). However, 10.♗d3 is second best (-0.11; 13).

10...   **f5?!**

The text looks risky. First of all, I had to check the game continuation. Black's weakening of his kingside and some of the central squares is overcome by his gain of space, command of e4, and refutation of the threat mentioned in the previous note. The computer likes 10...♕b6 with a slight pull for Black. 10...f5 is not listed among the seven best moves, although it is not a big mistake as its evaluation is near the seventh best and only about a third of a pawn worse than the best.

11.h3   **...**

The beginning of a faulty plan but the move is not bad in itself; in fact, *Rybka* rates it as best. White plans to kick the bishop by sacrificing his h- and g-pawns for Black's f-pawn, then "saccing" the bishop at h7 to regain it: i.e., 11...♗h5 12.g4 fxg4 13.hxg4 ♗xg4 14.♗xh7+ ♔xh7 15.♘g5+ ♔-any 16.♕xg4. But I had seen further. I gave this move a "?" but that is far from the truth.

11...   **♗h5**
12.g4?? −+   **...**

Here is the real culprit. White continues with this faulty plan. Better is 12.♗e2, when the computer has White somewhat better (0.22; 13).

12...   **fxg4**

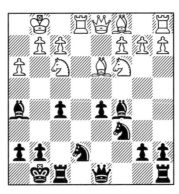

Position after 11...♗h4

13.hxg4(?)   **...**

White still does not know what is coming. After the game 13.♘g5 was analyzed (and it is best), but to no avail. The computer confirms that Black can simply get away with 13...♗xf2+ and 14...♗xe1 and White does not have nearly enough for the exchange.

13... **♗xg4**

The only way to fly. Suddenly it all dawns on White and he consumes about 25 minutes on his next move, which is forced, but all moves lose miserably.

14.♗e2 □ ...

Of course! White overlooked 14.♗xh7+ ♔h8! and wins. White would then have no way of protecting his knight on f3, a consequence of putting his other knight on c3 and, of course, moving his g-pawn. Now Black has an easy win. He is a pawn up with a better position and a far safer king. A simple win is obtained by maneuvering the queen to the kingside via d6 or e8, a plan I might adopt today. Similarly, *Rybka* prefers 14...♕c7 (−5.92; 13).

14... **♗xf2+!?**

The fun begins. White, of course, cannot refuse the sacrifice and has nothing to lose by accepting it, so he plays...

15.♔xf2 **♘e5**

Best by a long shot. Before 14...♗xf2+, I thought that 15...♘e5 would win back my piece immediately. Then, to my horror, I discovered the move 16.♗g5! with great complications, and the obvious lines turn out good for White when he sacrifices his queen, as will be seen! About 15 minutes later, to my dismay (and later joy because of the eventual complications), Mr. Yehl played...

16.♗g5! ...

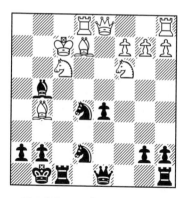

Position after 16.♗g5!

The best move from a practical standpoint, although every move loses by force. *Rybka's* best move, 16.♕d4, still leaves White behind by over four pawns after the simple 16...♗xf3 recovering the piece.

Now it was my turn to think and I did so for over half an hour, going over the one-hour mark. I wished that the time control was 16/2½! It seemed that I could study the position for hours on end and not come to a definite conclusion. Forty-one years later I can postulate that I was correct. In the other room friends Jerry Kolker and Lester Shelton were analyzing the position and, with moving the pieces(!), were having trouble comparing the relative merits of 16...♘xf3 and 16...♗xf3. I do not remember which one championed which move.

Formerly I had written, "The relative drawbacks of each are illustrated by the main variation of the position: 16...♘xf3 (or ♗xf3) 17.♗xf3! ♖xf3+ 18.♕xf3! ♗xf3 (or ♘xf3) 19.♗xe7 followed by ♔xf3. The resultant position is unclear. White has an exposed king, with rook, knight, and bishop for a queen and two connected passed pawns. I feel White should hold. However, this is only the main variation. At different points Black can interpose the check ...♕d8-b6+ and may manage to improve on the line. However, due to lack of space and the fascinating complexity of the position, I will leave it up to future generations to find the best lines after 16...♘xf3 or ...♗xf3. My move is more clearcut, although I didn't fully comprehend my plan at the time. Growing disgusted with the complications, I disgustedly played [16...♕b6+]..."

Well, it is two generations later and both moves are good but my move was best. For example, in the line given above, after 16...♘xf3 17.♗xf3, 17...♕b6+ does win easily.

16...   **♕b6+!!**

Now my knight is hanging. If White plays 17.♔f1, I leave my Knight hanging with 17... ♗h3#. I wrote "On 17.♔g2, things are unclear, but 17...♘xf3 looks winning." True, but 17...♖xf3 is even better, as the program *Zarkov 3* had seen almost twenty years ago.

17.♗e3   **...**

I had originally intended to answer the text with 17...♕e6, holding the d-pawn and probably regaining the piece on f3. However, it soon became apparent to me that I had a stronger, more forcing continuation.

17...   **♕f6!**

For all intents and purposes, this is the move that ends the struggle. Black threatens 18...♕h4+, which must be stopped, explaining White's reply. However, if White does allow Black to penetrate on the kingside, very beautiful lines occur. For instance, if White plays 18.♘xd5?, then 18...♕h4+ and *Rybka* announces mate in all lines, e.g.:

A) 19.♔g2 ♕h3+ 20.♔g1 ♘xf3+ 21.♗xf3 ♗xf3 22.♘xe7+ ♔h8 23.♕xf3 (23.♕d2 ♕h1+ 24.♔f2 ♕g2#) 23...♖xf3 etc.

B) 19.♔g1 ♛g3+ 20.♔h1 (20.♔f1 ♝h3#) 20...♝xf3+! 21.♝xf3:

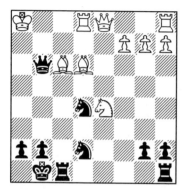

Position after 21.♝f3 (analysis)

21...♛h3+ (the original gave 21...♞xf3! but that just wins easily) 22.♔g1 ♞xf3+ 23.♛xf3 ♜xf3 and eventual mate.

18.♜h1   ...

This move is best, because White must give back a piece. However, it allows a nice finish. Other moves are also inadequate:

A) 18.♜g1 (to prevent the continuation actually played in the game) 18...♛h4+ 19.♜g3 ♝xf3 or 19...♞xf3 and White is helpless.

B) 18.♔g2 ♝xf3+ 19.♝xf3 ♛g6+ is a slaughter.

C) 18.♔g3 ♞f5+ 19.♔f2 ♞xe3 20.♔xe3 ♛b6+ 21.♛d4 ♞c4+ 22.♝xc4 ♜xf3+ and the queen falls.

D) 18.♔g1 or 18.♔f1 – Here Black can simply win back his piece with 18...♝xf3 and continue the attack.

White's busted.

18...   **♝xf3**

At last! Black will win back his piece. 18...♛e6 is also easily winning.

19.♝xf3   **♞g4+**

Or will he?! I could have played 19...♞xf3, but *Rybka* agrees the text is stronger and prettier, not to mention more forcing. White's queen appears to be lost.

20.♔e1   ...

A) 20.♔g1 leads to a line similar to the game: 20...♞xe3 21.♛e2 There is nothing better. 21...♛g5+ 22.♔f2 ♜xf3+ 23.♛xf3 (23.♔xf3 ♜f8#!) 23... ♜f8 wins the queen.

B) 20.♔g3 leads to a cute line 20...♘f5+! (see diagram below) 21.♔h3 (21.♔xg4 is "better" but loses the queen immediately to 21...♘xe3+) 21...♕h4+ 22.♔g2 ♘5xe3+ 23.♔g1 ♕f2#.

Position after 20...♘f5+! (analysis)

Now, finally, I do win back my piece – with interest.

| **20...** | **♘xe3** |
| **21.♘xd5** | **...** |

To answer 21...♘xd1 with 22.♘xf6+.

| **21...** | **♘7xd5** |
| **22.♗xd5+** | **♔h8** |

I took a while to play this. I wanted to make sure 23.♖xh7+ did not work. I did not wish to get swindled from my brilliancy. Of course 23.♖xh7+ ♔xh7 24.♕h5+ ♕h6 wins a rook for Black.

23.♕d2 **...**

White must stop 23...♕f2#. Objectively best is 23.♖xh7+ ♔xh7 24.♕h5+ ♕h6 25.♗e4+ ♔h8 but White has nothing for his rook sacrifice except a few more moves before resigning. (Subjectively best is Resigns.)

23... **♘xd5**

The best way to finish off White is 23...♖ae8, e.g. 24.c3 (what else?) ♘c4+ 25.♔d1 ♘xd2 winning the queen and then more.

24.♕xd5 **...**

Keeping material equal for one move. "Better" is 24.♕d3, when there follows 24...h6 – getting mated in such positions because one is only thinking offense is not the trait of a strong player – and then White can just resign or transpose into the game.

24...	♛f2+
25.♔d1	♜ad8
0-1	

It's a forced mate: 26.♛d3 ♜xd3+ 27.cxd3 ♛d4 28.♜h3 ♜f1+ 29.♔d2 ♛xb2+ 30.♔e3 ♛e5+ 31.♔d2 ♜f2+ 32.♔c1 ♛e1#.

Game 14: Kingside Attack!

An interesting tidbit: Over the years, every time I got a new computer I used this game as a benchmark of how much faster the software would find the key lines...

Don Latzel (1950) – Dan Heisman (1920)
Germantown Chess Club Ladder Game
Philadelphia 1970
Nimzo-Indian Defense
(50 moves in 2 hours)

1.d4	♞f6
2.c4	e6
3.♞c3	♝b4
4.e3	...

At the time, the most popular, Rubinstein Variation. Today 4.♛c2 is the most popular.

4...	b6

A move that was brought to my attention by the young British theoreticians.

5.♞e2	...

Most usual is 5.♝d3.

5...	♝a6
6.a3	♝e7
7.b3	...

The first deviation from standard play. 7.♞f4 is the normal move, and *Rybka* thinks it is slightly better than the 7.♞g3 that I reported Schwarz had criticized (in the first edition). After 7.b3 *Rybka* thinks the position is even.

7...	d5

Rybka slightly prefers castling, but by only 0.07 pawns at 15 ply.

8.♘f4   ...

Rybka thinks this is the only move which even gives White a small advantage (+0.12/14).

8...   **O-O** (10)

9.♗d3   ...

This move does not make the top three. At 14 ply, 9.♕f3 is best (+0.09).

9...   **dxc4**

10.bxc4   **♘bd7** (15)

It takes *Rybka* 12 ply before he likes this best, but at 14 ply it actually thinks Black is even (0.00/14).

11.O-O   ...

This and 11.♕a4 are equal best and...equal.

11...   **e5** (17)

Hmm. *Rybka* thinks I needed to play 11...c5 to keep equality. After 11...e5 the evaluation drops to 0.32 in favor of White at 13 ply. In Black's defense, I was purposely giving up the bishop pair.

12.♘4d5   ...

I did not expect this answer! But it is clearly best.

12...   **c5!** (22)

I gladly part with the two bishops. *Rybka* is not so sure and drops my evaluation to 0.43 in favor of White.

13.♘xe7+   **♕xe7**

14.d5   ...

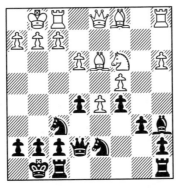

Position after 14.d5

The computer agrees that this is best, but only by a slight margin over 14.♖e1.

14...   **e4 (24)**

The only move which even keeps Black in the game. *Rybka* thinks all other moves are at least 0.3 pawns worse, and that is a lot!

15.♗e2   **♘e5 (25)**

Best again.

16.♕b3   **...**

In the first edition I wrote, "Apparently better than 16.♕a4," and it is: 16.♕b3 is (+.39/14) and 16.♕a4 is (0.26/14)! If only I could be that accurate all the time!

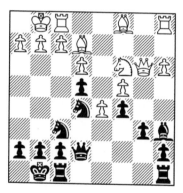

Position after 16.♕b3

16...   **♖ad8 (38)**

The first important move of the game – notice my time for the move. The reason I took so long (at 50 moves in 2 hours, 13 minutes is pretty long for me) is not that I was considering the alternative ...♗a6-c8, but that I was trying to develop my game plan. As it turns out, *Rybka* thinks that 16...♗c8 is best (+0.38/14) and that 16...♖ad8 doesn't make its top three!

My original idea stared me in the face: get the knight on f6 to d6 in order to first blockade the passed pawn and secondly put great pressure on White's c-pawn. However, there is no tactical justification to such a maneuver: 16...♘e8? 17.♘xe4 and now 17...♘xc4 loses a piece to 18.♗xc4 ♕xe4 19.♗xa6. So, the problem becomes: What else can I do? Certainly 16...♖ad8 detracts from my queenside defense. The black queen's rook later participates in some lines of play that occur only in the notes.

However, the same job can be done by 16...♖fd8, which is therefore better than the text. The reason is that after White plays a4-a5, I can play my rook on a8 to c8 after playing ...bxa5. Then after ♖xa5 for White, I will have my Bishop removed as in the game and White's queenside attack is less potent. Another possibility is that I will try to hold my a- or b-pawns with my queen and rook. Yet another possible move is 16... ♗c8, resulting in lines similar to the game, but with "a little less attack on both sides." Maybe 16...♗c8 is good, but it would probably have been a lot less exciting.

17.a4 ...

In order to reach his full advantage, White should play 17.h3 (0.55/13). That stops future kingside play in its tracks – and would have prevented this game from getting in the book...

However, after 17.a4, White is still ahead (0.53/12) so it is just about as good! Credit to Don.

17... **♗c8** (46)

A valuable eight minutes. In this nothing-to-lose club game, I now smell white king blood and I'm determined to pull off a kingside attack. And, as Kavalek would say, "with a little help from my friends" [a reference to a *Chess Life* article GM Lubomir Kavalek wrote around this time] – it works great. *Rybka* thinks that 17...♘fg4 is objectively best, but that is (0.52/13) so I am in danger in any case.

18.a5 ...

In the first edition I wrote, "Having said "a," or rather a4, White now says "b," a5. Certainly after 17.a4, 18.a5 is best." Results at 13 ply: 18.a5 is (0.69/13) – the second-best move, 18.♗b2 is (0.52/13) so I get an "A" for that comment.

18... **♘6g4?!** (54)

I am going for the gusto, but it really is not there. Objectively best is the meek 18...bxa5 (0.54/13), but against a human my idea is very dangerous.

19.axb6(?) ...

Starting at this point just letting the computer run with deep searches is not always enough to get toward the truth. Better is to force the computer down analysis lines and see what it finds. Apparently here White has two good lines: 19.♘xe4 (the move suggested in the first edition) and the dangerous-looking 19.h3. Everything else is equal or worse. Let's consider the principal variation (PV) of each:

19.♘xe4 ♘xh2 (nothing else is close) 20.♔xh2 ♕h4+ 21.♔g1 ♕xe4 22.axb6 axb6 23.♕xb6 ♘xc4 24.♕xc5 and White is in command.

19.h3!? ♘f6 (19...♘f3+ 20.gxf3 +−) 20.axb6 axb6, and now not 21.♕xb6 ♗xh3!? 22.gxh3 ♘f3+ 23.♗xf3 exf3 24.e4 ♖d6 with attack, but 21.♖a3 and if 21...♗xh3 22.gxh3 ♘f3+ 23.♗xf3 exf3 24.e4 and White is winning.

19...	♘f3+! (60)

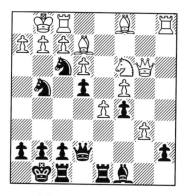

Position after 19...♘f3+!

In the first edition I wrote, "Only! This apparently came as a surprise to White. No use analyzing other moves for Black." Unfortunately this is not correct. Black has two other tries in 19...♕h4 and 19...♘xh2. Of these 19...♕h4 is the key, so let's analyze that: 19...♕h4. Now 20.h3 does fail to 20...♘f3+, e.g. 21.♗xf3 exf3 22.♘d1 (the pattern 22.hxg4 ♕xg4 23.g3 ♕h3 with inevitable mate is a good one to know) 22...fxg2 23.♔xg2 ♘e5 24.e4 ♖d6 25.♖a3 ♖xb6 and Black wins easily. So the main defense is 20.♗xg4, with a possible continuation 20...♗xg4 21.f3 exf3 and Black is much better, likely winning, e.g. 22.g3 ♕h3 23.♖a2 axb6, when neither 24.♕xb8 ♖a8 nor 24.e4 ♖a8 seem to completely save White.

20.♗xf3	...

In the first edition I wrote "Forced. Both 20.gxf3 and 20.♔h1 meet with rapid disaster." This is true:

A) 20.gxf3 allows mate in 8, e.g. 20...exf3 21.♗xf3 ♕h4 22.h3 ♕xh3 23.♗xg4 ♕xg4+ 24.♔h2 ♖d6 25.e4 ♕h3+ 26.♔g1 ♖g6+ 27.♗g5 ♖xd6#.

B) 20.♔h1 allows mate in 6, e.g. 20...♕d6 21.g3 ♕h6 22.h4 ♘xh4 23.♗xg4 ♘f3+ 24.♗h5 ♕xh5+ 25.♔g2 ♕h3#.

20...	exf3
21.h3?	...

In the first edition I wrote, "A hard decision. White foresees that h2-h3 will undoubtedly be necessary in the near future so he decides to play it now, hoping the knight will retreat. White has four tries other than 21.h3: A) 21.g3, B) 21.♘e4, C) 21.gxf3, and D) 21.bxa7!" Of these the best is 21.g3, but it turns out the best defense may be 21.b7!?. Let's analyze both of these:

A) 21.g3 ♘xh2 22.b7 ♕g5 23.bxc8♕ ♕h5 24.♘e4 ♘xf1 25.♘f6+ gxf6 26.♕g4+ ♕xg4 27.♔xf1 ♕h3+ 28.♔e1 ♕h1+ 29.♔d2 ♕g2, and Black is winning easily.

B) 21.b7 To deflect the bishop from guarding h3. 21...♗xb7 and now White has either 22.g3 or 22.h3:

B1) 22.g3 ♘e5 23.h3 ♕d7 24.g4 ♕e7, when 25...♕h4 is unstoppable, e.g. 25.♔h2 ♕h4 26.♖g1 ♕xf2+.

B2) 22.h3 fxg2 (22...♘e5 23.e4 ♗c8 24.♖e1 24.♘e2!? [24...♗xh3 25.g3 ♕d7 26.♕b5 ♕c8 and the threat of ...♗f1 and ...♕h3, with mate on g2, wins] 24...fxe2 25.♖e1 ♖d6 26.f4 ♘g6 27.♖xe2 ♖f6 and Black should win, although there is some play for White) 23.♔xg2 ♕g5 24.e4 ♘e3+ 25.♔f3 ♕g2+ 26.♔xe3 ♕xf1, and Black is winning.

21...   **♕h4** (76)

21...fxg2 22.♔xg2 ♕h4 also wins but the game continuation is even more accurate.

22.♘e4   **...**

In the original annotations I wrote that, "Nothing saves the day." That is true. A small sample of alternatives:

A) 22.b7 fxg2 23.♔xg2 ♘xe3+ 24.fxe3 ♗xh3+ 25.♔f3 ♗xf1 26.♗a3 ♗xc4 −+.

B) 22.♘d1 (as good as any) 22...♘e5 23.e4 ♗xh3 24.g3 ♕h5 25.♘e3 ♗xf1 −+.

22...   **fxg2** (78)

That took only two minutes. White's reply is forced.

23.♔xg2   **♘e5** (81)

Best again. Now the win becomes clearer.

24.f4   **...**

The only other defense, 24.f3, fails to 24...♗xh3+ 25.♔g1 ♖d6!. *Rybka* confirms this is a forced mate in 8 starting with Black's 24th move.

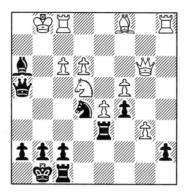

Position after 25...♖d6! (analysis)

24...   **♗xh3+**

The waters clear. White is (has been) dead.

25.♔g1   **♕g4+**

The queen now penetrates. 26.♔f2 ♕g2+ picks up the rook next move with check yet, so...

0-1

About the Author

Dan Heisman attended Caltech and Penn State, receiving a Master's degree in Engineering Science. In 1972 his team won the U.S. Amateur Team Championship. In 1973 Mr. Heisman won the Philadelphia Closed Invitational Championship and in 1971 and 1976 the Philadelphia Open Championships. Mr. Heisman holds the titles of National Master from the U.S. Chess Federation and Candidate Master from FIDE, the international chess federation. Since 1996 Mr. Heisman has been a full-time chess instructor and author. His other nine chess books include *Elements of Positional Evaluation, Everyone's 2nd Chess Book, A Parent's Guide to Chess, Looking for Trouble, The Improving Annotator*, and Back *to Basics: Tactics*. His No*vice* No*ok* column at Chess Café has won numerous annual awards for Best Instruction from the Chess Journalists of America, and in 2005 it received the organization's prestigious Cramer Award for Outstanding Column in any Media. Mr. Heisman's question-and-answer show aired weekly for years on the Internet Chess Club's (ICC) chess.FM radio station, and recently he has created dozens of instructional videos for the ICC. Radio personality Howard Stern is among his many students. Mr. Heisman currently lives with his wife Shelly in Wynnewood, Pennsylvania, and can be contacted via his informative website, www.danheisman.com.

Notes